QUILT-LOVERS' FAVORITES™

FROM AMERICAN PATCHWORK & QUILTING®

Better Homes and Gardens® Creative Collection™
Des Moines, Iowa

VOLUME 2

Better Homes and Gardens®

QUILT-LOVERS' FAVORITES™

FROM AMERICAN PATCHWORK & QUILTING®

Editor-in-Chief BEVERLY RIVERS

Executive Editor HEIDI KAISAND	*Art Director* PATRICIA CHURCH PODLASEK
Senior Editor	JENNIFER KELTNER
Associate Art Director	MELISSA GANSEN BEAUCHAMP
Administrative Assistant	MARY IRISH

Contributing Editor JILL ABELOE MEAD
Contributing Graphic Designer BARBARA J. GORDON
Contributing Copy Editors DIANE DORO, JENNIFER SPEER RAMUNDT, AND DEBRA MORRIS SMITH
Quilt Tester LAURA BOEHNKE
Technical Editor LILA SCOTT
Contributing Watercolor Illustrator ANN WEISS
Contributing Technical Illustrator CHRIS NEUBAUER GRAPHICS

Publisher MAUREEN RUTH
Consumer Products Marketing Director BEN JONES
Consumer Products Marketing Manager KARRIE NELSON
Associate Business Director CRAIG FEAR
Production Director DOUGLAS M. JOHNSTON
Book Production Managers PAM KVITNE
MARJORIE J. SCHENKELBERG
Marketing Assistant CHERYL ECKERT

Vice President Publishing Director WILLIAM R. REED

Meredith CORPORATION

Chairman and CEO WILLIAM T. KERR

Chairman of the Executive Committee E.T. MEREDITH III

Meredith Publishing Group
President STEPHEN M. LACY
Magazine Group President JERRY KAPLAN
Creative Services ELLEN DE LATHOUDER
Manufacturing BRUCE HESTON
Consumer Marketing KARLA JEFFRIES
Finance and Administration MAX RUNCIMAN

ISSN: 1532-8848   ISBN: 0-696-21511-X

For book editorial questions, write:
Better Homes and Gardens Quilt-Lovers' Favorites • *1716 Locust St., GA-305, Des Moines, IA 50309-3023*

TREASURED QUILTS

Favorite quilt patterns endure the test of time. No matter how many generations have treasured them, these designs continue to bring a twinkle to the eye. Such is the case with the quilts in this second volume of Quilt-Lovers' Favorites™. *The book's 15 main projects, pulled from the pages of* American Patchwork & Quilting® *magazine, are patterns regularly requested and tested by the readers. We know they're popular because they're the projects most often seen in our "Quilts & Quotes" section, and they're the ones readers ask for time and time again.*

To entice you to take a fresh look at these favorite quilts, we've created dozens of brand-new projects using blocks, units, or appliqué patterns from the original quilts as inspiration. You'll find projects suitable for every room in the house and some for you to wear or take along when you travel. And, of course, we've provided optional size charts for each of the main projects so you can make almost every quilt in any size you choose.

We hope you enjoy this timeless collection of quilts—you know they're the Quilt-Lovers' *Favorites.*

Heidi Kaisand

Executive Editor, American Patchwork & Quilting®

TABLE *of* CONTENTS

CHERISHED CLASSICS
Page **6**

SIMPLE SENSATIONS
Page **30**

8 TIMELESS TREASURE
11 Optional Sizes
12 Patchwork Stocking
13 Patchwork Cuff Stocking
15 Two-Color Throw

16 CROWN OF THORNS
21 Framed Sunflower
22 Tabletop Quilt

24 CANDY STRIPES
27 Optional Sizes
27 Pillowcase
28 Jungle Wall Hanging

32 CHECKMATE
35 Optional Sizes
36 Duvet Cover
38 Wall Quilt

40 ENGLISH TRELLIS
44 Optional Sizes
44 Batik Quilt
46 Checkerboard

48 LUMBERJACK
52 Optional Sizes
52 Kid's Flannel Brights Quilt
54 Picnic Cloth

COLORFUL CREATIONS
Page **56**

STAR ATTRACTIONS
Page **90**

ALL ABOUT APPLIQUE
Page **118**

58 THERE GOES THE NEIGHBORHOOD
64 Optional Sizes
65 House Pillow
67 Anniversary Quilt

70 COLORFUL CAKES
74 Optional Sizes
74 Tea Tray
76 Tea Cozy
78 Signature Quilt

80 DURANGO PINWHEEL
84 Optional Sizes
85 Quilted Tablecloth
86 Chair Quilt
88 Baby Quilt

92 AMERICAN BEAUTY
95 Optional Sizes
96 Double Ruffle Pillow
98 Single Ruffle Pillow
99 Appliqué Jacket
100 Shower Curtain

102 AUNT MAGGIE'S QUILT
106 Optional Sizes
106 Christmas Tree Skirt
109 Travel Bag

110 STAR CHAIN
114 Optional Sizes
114 Mini Quilt
116 Sheet Set
117 Pillowcases

120 SOWN FABRIC
126 Row Quilt
128 Appliqué Dress and Jacket

130 I LOVE YOU
133 Grandmother's Handprint Quilt
134 Gift Bag & Tag

136 BELLA TULIP GARDEN
142 Window Valance
144 Embroidered Tea Towel

145 QUILTER'S SCHOOLHOUSE
145 Getting Started
146 Cutting with Templates
148 Rotary Cutting
150 Piecing
152 Appliqué
154 Quilting
157 Covered Cording
157 Cutting Bias Strips
158 Hanging Sleeves
159 Finishing

160 CREDITS

CHERISHED CLASSICS

Traditional quilt patterns have remained popular over the centuries for many reasons, not the least of which is their practicality. These familiar designs can be endlessly remade in as many ways as you can imagine. With a variety of different fabrics—from scraps to specialty prints—you can make a tried-and-true pattern look as antique or as contemporary as you desire.

TIMELESS
Treasure

With inspiration from a traditional block and the multitude of

reproduction fabrics available today, project designer Mabeth Oxenreider

created this dynamic bed-size quilt.

Materials

11½ yards total of assorted light, medium, and

    dark prints for blocks (see Select the Fabrics)

⅝ yard of red print for binding

9½ yards of backing fabric

90×114" of quilt batting

Finished quilt top: 84×108"
Finished block: 6" square

Quantities specified for 44/45"-wide, 100% cotton
fabrics. All measurements include a ¼" seam
allowance. Sew with right sides together unless
otherwise stated.

Select the Fabrics

While the piecing of this quilt top is relatively
simple, gathering the variety of fabric scraps that
project designer Mabeth Oxenreider used could take
a while. That's why the yardage requirement for the
quilt top is specified as a total amount (see Materials)
rather than being identified by fabric color.

Mabeth chose prints with lots of texture, value,
and scale. She suggests avoiding tone-on-tone prints,
as they appear solid from a distance. Mabeth used
light shirtings and plaids in blue, pink, and gold for
the Four-Patch units. She found that reproduction
fabrics work well.

A total of 252 Triple Four-Patch blocks compose
this quilt. One Triple Four-Patch block is composed
of two Four-Patch blocks plus two 3½" squares.
Chain piecing can speed up the process.

For one Triple Four-Patch block, you'll need two
3½" squares and four 2" squares from the same print,
if possible, plus eight light print and eight dark print
1¼" squares. To get these pieces, Mabeth cut a

continued

3½×42" strip from a variety of fabrics. From each strip, she first cut six 3½" squares. Next she cut the strips down to 2" wide, then cut the narrower strips into 2" squares. Each strip gave her enough pieces for two blocks. She mixed and matched the extras at the end to create more blocks. A 5½×8" rectangle will result in enough fabric for all the 3½" and 2" squares needed for one block.

Mabeth was more repetitive when making the Four-Patch units, using the strip-piecing technique to cut and assemble them. The instructions under Cut the Fabrics reflect this.

Cut the Fabrics

To make the best use of your fabrics, cut the pieces in the order that follows. The term "sets" indicates pieces that are cut from the same fabric.

From light prints, cut:
- 63—1¼×42" strips

From medium and dark prints, cut:
- 63—1¼×42" strips
- 252 sets of four 2" squares and two 3½" squares

From red print, cut:
- 10—2×42" binding strips

Assemble the Four-Patch Units

1. Aligning long edges, sew together a light print 1¼×42" strip and a medium or dark print 1¼×42" strip to make a strip set. Press the seam allowance toward the darker strip (see Diagram 1). Cut the strip set into thirty-two 1¼"-wide segments.

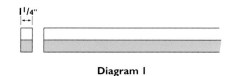

Diagram 1

2. Lay out two Step 1 segments as shown in Diagram 2. Sew together the segments to make a Four-Patch unit. The pieced Four-Patch unit should measure 2" square, including the seam allowances. Repeat to make a total of 16 Four-Patch units.

Diagram 2

3. Repeat steps 1 and 2 until you've made a total of 252 sets of four Four-Patch units.

Note: To speed up the cutting and piecing of the Four-Patch units, Mabeth suggests using the strip-piecing technique. After assembling a strip set, cut it in half. Layer the two halves with right sides together, making sure the light strip from one half is atop the dark strip from the other half (see Diagram 3). Because the seam allowances are pressed toward the dark strip, they are now in opposite directions, causing the two halves to "lock" in place. Cut the layered strip set into 1¼"-wide segments; then sew the layered segments together to make Four-Patch units. Carefully handle the segments as you move them to the sewing machine so you don't "unlock" the seams.

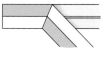

Diagram 3

Assemble the Four-Patch Blocks

1. To make a Four-Patch block, lay out two matching Four-Patch units and two matching 2" squares (see Diagram 4, noting the placement of the light squares in the Four-Patch units). Sew together the squares in each row. Press the seam allowances toward the 2" squares. Join the rows to make a Four-Patch block. Press the seam allowance in either direction. The pieced Four-Patch block should measure 3½" square, including the seam allowances.

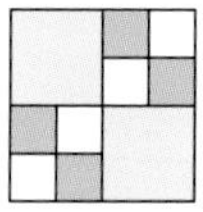

Diagram 4

2. Repeat to make a total of 252 sets of two Four-Patch blocks each.

Assemble the Triple Four-Patch Blocks

1. To make a Triple Four-Patch block, lay out two matching Four-Patch blocks and two 3½" squares that match the 2" squares in the blocks (see Diagram 5 *opposite*). Sew together the squares in each row. Press the seam allowances toward the 3½" squares. Join the rows to make a Triple Four-Patch block. Press the seam allowance in either direction. The pieced block should measure 6½" square, including the seam allowances.

Diagram 5

2. Repeat Step 1 to make a total of 252 Triple Four-Patch blocks.

Assemble the Quilt Top

Referring to the photograph at *right*, lay out the 252 blocks in 18 horizontal rows. Sew together the blocks in each row. Press the seam allowances in one direction, alternating the direction with each row. Then join the rows to complete the quilt top. Press the seam allowances in one direction.

Complete the Quilt

1. Layer the quilt top, batting, and backing according to the instructions in Quilter's Schoolhouse, which begins on *page 145*. Hand- or machine-quilt as desired.

2. Use the red print 2×42" strips to bind the quilt according to the instructions in Quilter's Schoolhouse.

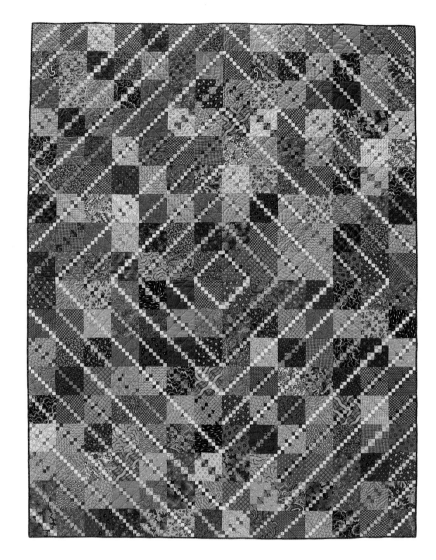

Timeless Treasure Quilt
optional sizes

If you'd like to make this quilt in a size other than for a double bed, use the information *below*.

Alternate quilt sizes	Crib/Lap	Twin	King
Number of blocks	63	140	361
Number of blocks wide by long	7×9	10×14	19×19
Finished size	42×54"	60×84"	114" square
Yardage requirements			
Total of assorted light, medium, and dark prints	3¼ yards	7 yards	18 yards
Binding	⅓ yard	½ yard	⅔ yard
Backing	2⅔ yards	5⅓ yards	10 yards
Batting	48×60"	66×96"	120" square

PATCHWORK STOCKING

Create a miniature quilt first, then cut your stocking pattern out of it. It's the perfect way to showcase your hobby for the holidays.

Materials

Scraps of assorted green prints for blocks

Scraps of assorted red prints for blocks

16×24" rectangle of muslin for backing

⅝ yard of coordinating print for stocking back and lining

⅓ yard of dark green print for cording cover

¾ yard of ¼"-diameter cotton cording

16×24" rectangle of quilt batting

Finished block: 6" square

Cut the Fabrics

To make the best use of your fabrics, cut the pieces in the order that follows. The term "sets" indicates pieces that are cut from the same fabric.

From assorted green prints, cut:
- 48—1¼" squares

From assorted red prints, cut:
- 6 sets of four 2" squares and two 3½" squares
- 48—1¼" squares

From dark green print, cut:
- 1—12" square, cutting it into enough 1½"-wide bias strips to total 30" in length (For specific instructions on cutting bias strips, see Quilter's Schoolhouse, which begins on *page 145.*)

From the ¼"-diameter cording, cut:
- 1—20" piece
- 1—7" piece

Assemble the Blocks

1. Referring to Diagram 2 on *page 10,* lay out two green print 1¼" squares and two red print 1¼" squares. Sew together the squares in pairs, then join the pairs to make a Four-Patch unit. The Four-Patch unit should measure 2" square, including the seam allowances. Repeat to make a total of six sets of two Four-Patch units.

2. Referring to the Assemble the Four-Patch Blocks instructions on *page 10,* use the Four-Patch units from Step 1 *above* and the assorted red print 2" squares to make a total of six sets of two Four-Patch blocks.

3. Referring to Assemble the Triple Four-Patch Blocks instructions on *page 10,* use the Four-Patch blocks from Step 2 *above* and the assorted red print 3½" squares to make a total of six Triple Four-Patch blocks.

Assemble the Patchwork

1. Referring to the left stocking in the photograph *opposite* for placement, lay out the Triple Four-Patch blocks in three horizontal rows. Sew together the blocks in each row. Press the seam allowances in one direction, alternating the direction with each row. Then join the rows. Press the seam allowances in one direction. The patchwork piece should measure 12½×18½", including the seam allowances.

2. Layer the patchwork piece, batting, and muslin according to the instructions in Quilter's Schoolhouse, which begins on *page 145.*

3. Quilt as desired. This patchwork was hand-quilted in diagonal rows. Trim the batting and muslin even with the quilted patchwork.

Assemble the Stocking

The stocking pattern is on *Pattern Sheet 1.* To make a template of the pattern, follow the instructions in Quilter's Schoolhouse.

From patchwork, cut:
- 1 of Stocking Pattern

From coordinating print for stocking back and lining, cut:
- 1 of Stocking Pattern
- 2 of Stocking Pattern reversed

1. With right sides together, join the patchwork stocking piece and a coordinating print stocking reversed piece, leaving the top edge open, to make the stocking. Turn right side out; press.

2. With right sides together, join the remaining coordinating print stocking and stocking reversed pieces, leaving the top edge and a 4" space in the bottom of the foot open, to make the stocking lining. Do *not* turn the lining right side out; press.

3. Using the dark green print bias strips and the cording, create a 20" length of covered cording. (For specific instructions on making covered cording, see Quilter's Schoolhouse.)

4. With raw edges aligned, sew together the covered cording and the stocking; begin stitching 1½" from the cording's finished end.

5. Cut the exposed end of the cording so that it fits snugly into the finished end. The ends of the cording should abut inside the cording cover. Stitch the ends in place and trim the raw edges as needed.

6. With the right side out, wrap the remaining dark green print 1½×7" bias strip around the 7" piece of cording. Turn the long edge under ¼" and slip-stitch the folded edge over the raw edge. Fold the covered cording in half to create a hanging loop. Pin the hanging loop ends to the right side of the stocking at the seam line.

7. Right sides together, slip the stocking into the stocking lining (the lining will be wrong side out with the seams showing). Sew together the top edges of the stocking and the stocking lining, with the cording seam allowance and hanging loop between the layers. Turn right side out through the opening in the foot. Whipstitch the lining foot opening closed. Push the stocking lining into position inside the stocking to complete the project.

PATCHWORK CUFF STOCKING

For a classic look, top off your holiday

stocking with a quilted cuff created from the

"Timeless Treasure" quilt pattern.

Materials

Scraps of red print for blocks

Scraps of green print for blocks

7×16" rectangle of muslin for backing

⅝ yard of mottled red print for stocking front, lining, and back

½ yard of green holiday print for cording cover

2⅜ yards of ¼"-diameter cotton cording

7×16" rectangle of quilt batting

continued

Finished block: 2" square

Cut the Fabrics

To make the best use of your fabrics, cut the pieces in the order that follows.

From green print, cut:
- 12—1½" squares
- 1—1×27" strip

From red print, cut:
- 24—1½" squares
- 1—1×27" strip

From green print, cut:
- 1—18" square, cutting it into enough 1½"-wide bias strips to total 85" in length (For specific instructions on cutting bias strips, see Quilter's Schoolhouse, which begins on *page 145*.)

Assemble the Blocks

1. Referring to the Assemble the Four-Patch Units instructions on *page 10*, use the green print 1×27" strip and red print 1×27" strip to make a total of 12 Four-Patch units. Each pieced Four-Patch unit should measure 1½" square, including the seam allowances.

2. Referring to the Assemble the Four-Patch Blocks instructions on *page 10*, use the small Four-Patch units from Step 1 *above* and 12 red print 1½" squares to make a total of six Four-Patch blocks. Each pieced Four-Patch block should measure 2½" square, including the seam allowances.

3. Use the 12 green print 1½" squares and the remaining 12 red print 1½" squares to make a total of six variation Four-Patch blocks as shown in Diagram 1. Each variation Four-Patch block should measure 2½" square, including the seam allowances.

Diagram 1

Assemble and Complete the Patchwork Cuff

1. Referring to the right stocking in the photograph on *page 13*, lay out the blocks in two horizontal rows, alternating the Four-Patch blocks and the variation Four-Patch blocks. Join the blocks in rows, pressing the seam allowances in each row in opposite directions. Sew together the rows, pressing the seam allowance to one side to make a patchwork piece. The patchwork piece should measure 4½×12½", including the seam allowances.

2. Layer the patchwork piece, batting, and muslin according to the instructions in Quilter's Schoolhouse.

3. Quilt as desired. Trim the batting and muslin even with the quilted patchwork.

4. Using the green print 1½"-wide bias strips and the cording, create an 85" length of covered cording. (For specific instructions on making covered cording, see Quilter's Schoolhouse.)

5. Cut the covered cording into the following lengths: 44", 20", 12½", and 7".

6. With raw edges aligned, sew the 12½" piece of covered cording to one 12½" edge of the embroidered patchwork piece to complete the cuff.

Assemble the Stocking

The stocking pattern is on *Pattern Sheet 1*. To make a template of the pattern, follow the instructions in Quilter's Schoolhouse.

From mottled red print, cut:
- 1—12½×14½" rectangle for stocking front
- 1 of Stocking Pattern
- 2 of Stocking Pattern reversed

1. With raw edges aligned, sew together the corded edge of the cuff and one short edge of the mottled red print 12½×14½" rectangle.

2. Cut one Stocking Pattern from the cuffed rectangle to create the stocking front.

3. With raw edges aligned, sew the 44" piece of covered cording to the outer edge of the stocking front.

4. Using the remaining covered cording pieces from Step 5 *above*, refer to the Assemble the Stocking instructions on *page 12* to complete the stocking.

TWO-COLOR THROW

Choose fabrics from a two-color palette for

a less scrappy twist on the original quilt.

Materials

5/8 yard total of assorted yellow print scraps
   for blocks

1 3/4 yards total of assorted light blue and blue print
   scraps for blocks

1/3 yard of blue print for binding

2 2/3 yards of backing fabric

48" square of quilt batting

Finished quilt top: 42" square
Finished block: 6" square

Cut the Fabrics

To make the best use of your fabrics, cut the pieces
in the order that follows. The term "sets" indicates
pieces that are cut from the same fabric.

From assorted yellow prints, cut:
• 13—1¼×42" strips

From assorted light blue and blue prints, cut:
• 49 sets of four 2" squares and two 3½" squares
• 13—1¼×42" strips

From blue print, cut:
• 5—2×42" binding strips

Assemble the Blocks

1. Referring to the Assemble the Four-Patch
   instructions on *page 10*, use the 14 assorted
   yellow print 1½×42" strips and the 14 assorted
   blue print 1½×42" strips to make a total of 49 sets
   of two Four-Patch units.

2. Referring to the Assemble the Four-Patch Blocks
   instructions on *page 10*, use the Four-Patch units

from Step 1 *above* and the assorted blue print
2" squares to make a total of 49 sets of two
Four-Patch blocks.

3. Referring to Assemble the Triple Four-Patch
   Blocks instructions on *page 10*, use the Four-Patch
   blocks from Step 2 *above* and the assorted blue
   print 3½" squares to make a total of 49 Triple
   Four-Patch blocks.

Assemble the Quilt Top

Lay out the Triple Four-Patch blocks in seven
horizontal rows, arranging the blocks so that the
yellow squares are in diagonal rows. Sew together
the blocks in each row. Press the seam allowances in
one direction, alternating the direction with each
row. Then join the rows to complete the quilt top.
Press the seam allowances in one direction.

Complete the Quilt

1. Layer the quilt top, batting, and backing according
   to the instructions in Quilter's Schoolhouse, which
   begins on *page 145*.

2. Quilt as desired. This quilt was hand-quilted in
   diagonal rows.

3. Use the blue print 2×42" strips to bind the
   quilt according to the instructions in Quilter's
   Schoolhouse.

CROWN OF *Thorns*

Quiltmaker Nora Cope enjoys nothing better than mixing selections

from her collection of Asian-print fabrics into a quilt top. In this large quilt,

she combines the colorful fabrics in a traditional pieced block.

Materials

3 yards total of assorted dark Asian prints
   for blocks

1¾ yards total of assorted light Asian prints
   for blocks

2 yards total of assorted neutral prints for blocks

2 yards of bright blue print for sashing and
   inner border

⅛ yard of solid red-orange for sashing

2 yards of red-and-blue Asian print for outer
   border and binding

¼ yard of gold Asian print for outer border

⅝ yard total of assorted blue and dark blue
   Asian prints for outer border

⅜ yard of assorted red Asian prints for
   outer border

4 yards of backing fabric

70×84" of quilt batting

Finished quilt top: 63¾×78¼"
Finished block: 6¾" square

Quantities specified for 44/45"-wide, 100% cotton
fabrics. All measurements include a ¼" seam
allowance. Sew with right sides together unless
otherwise stated.

continued

Foundation-Piecing Method

Designer Nora Cope foundation-pieced the arcs in this quilt, which means she stitched the pieces together on paper patterns, then tore off the paper once the arcs were complete.

For foundation piecing, you need paper patterns, called foundation papers, and fabric pieces that are at least ¼" larger on all sides than the areas they are to cover. *Note:* Cutting generous fabric pieces will reduce the chance for assembly errors.

Because the fabric pieces are sewn directly to the foundation papers, which provide support, there's no need to consider grain lines when cutting fabric pieces. And the fabric pieces don't have to be cut perfectly. You'll trim the pieces to the correct size after stitching them to the foundation papers.

To foundation-piece an arc, set your sewing machine's stitch length to 12 to 16 stitches per inch, which will allow the foundation paper to easily tear away from the assembled arc. Layer two fabric pieces with right sides together.

With the right side of a foundation paper facing up, place the layered fabric pieces under the designated areas of the foundation paper. Then, with the foundation paper still on top, machine-stitch on the designated seam line that joins the two fabric pieces, sewing through all three layers. Press the pieces open and trim only the fabric pieces (not the foundation paper) to the size indicated on the pattern, leaving ¼" around each piece for seam allowances. Continue adding fabric pieces in numerical order until the arc is completed.

Trace the Foundation Papers

Lay a piece of tracing paper over the Block Arc Pattern on *Pattern Sheet 1*. With a sharp pencil or fine-tip quilter's pen and ruler, transfer all lines and numbers from the pattern to the tracing paper. (We suggest tracing because some photocopy machines can alter proportions.) Repeat to make a total of 48 foundation-paper arcs.

Cut the Fabrics

To make the best use of your fabrics, cut the pieces in the order that follows. The patterns are on *Pattern Sheet 1*. To make templates of the patterns, follow the instructions in Quilter's Schoolhouse, which begins on *page 145*.

Cut the border strips the length of the fabric (parallel to the selvage). The measurements for the border strips are mathematically correct. You may wish to cut your border strips longer than specified to allow for possible sewing differences.

From assorted dark Asian prints, cut:
- 48 *each* of patterns A and B
- 320—2¼×3" rectangles for foundation piecing (you'll need 32 sets of 7 matching dark print rectangles and 16 sets of 6 matching dark print rectangles)

From assorted light Asian prints, cut:
- 304—2¼×3" rectangles for foundation piecing (you'll need 32 sets of 6 matching light print rectangles and 16 sets of 7 matching light print rectangles)

From assorted neutral prints, cut:
- 48 *each* of patterns C and C reversed

From bright blue print, cut:
- 2—1½×63" inner border strips
- 2—1½×48" inner border strips
- 17—1½×14" sashing strips
- 14—1½×7¼" sashing strips

From solid red-orange, cut:
- 12—1½" squares for sashing

From red-and-blue Asian print, cut:
- 4—9⅝×46½" strips for outer border
- 8—2½×42" binding strips

From gold Asian print, cut:
- 2—2½×27½" strips for outer border
- 2—2½×20½" strips for outer border

From assorted blue and dark blue Asian prints, cut:
- 10—5⅞" squares, cutting each in half diagonally to make a total of 20 large triangles for outer border
- 2—6¼" squares, cutting each diagonally twice in an X to make a total of 8 small triangles for outer border

From assorted red Asian prints, cut:
- 12—5½" squares for outer border

Foundation-Piece the Arcs

1. For one arc you'll need seven matching dark print 2¼×3" rectangles and six matching light print 2¼×3" rectangles. With right sides together, place a dark print rectangle atop a light print rectangle. Put a foundation paper on top of the dark print rectangle (see Diagram 1). Position the layered rectangles a scant ¼" beyond stitching

Diagram 1

line No. 1 and about ⅜" above the top of the arc. Sew on stitching line No. 1.

2. If necessary, trim only the seam allowance (not the paper) to a scant ¼". Press open the rectangles (see Diagram 2). Trim the light print rectangle about ¼" beyond sewing line No. 2 (see Diagram 3). Trim both fabric pieces even with the outer edges of the foundation paper.

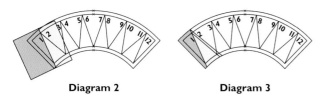

Diagram 2   **Diagram 3**

3. With right sides together, layer another dark print rectangle with the trimmed edge of the light print piece. Sew along stitching line No. 2. Press the pieces open. Trim the dark print rectangle to about ¼" beyond sewing line No. 3 and even with the outer edges of the foundation paper (see Diagram 4).

Diagram 4

4. Continue adding light and dark print rectangles to the foundation paper in the same manner until you've pieced the entire arc. Then, with the blunt edge of a seam ripper, remove the foundation paper from the pieced arc.

5. Repeat steps 1 through 4 to make a total of 32 pieced arcs that start and end with dark prints. In the same manner, make a total of 16 pieced arcs that start and end with light prints.

Assemble the Crown of Thorns Blocks

1. For one Crown of Thorns block you'll need one pieced arc, one dark print A piece, one dark print B piece, one neutral print C piece, and one neutral print C reversed piece.

2. With right sides together and the center marks aligned, place the dark print B piece atop the dark print A piece. First pin the pieces together at the center mark, then pin each end. Finish by pinning generously in between. (When pinning curved seams such as this one, use slender pins

and pick up only a few threads at each position.) Sew together the dark print A and B pieces, removing each pin just before your needle reaches it, to make an A/B unit. Press the seam toward the dark print B piece.

3. Pin the A/B unit to the inner edge of the pieced arc (see the Block Assembly Diagram), matching the center mark on the dark print A piece with the center mark on the pieced arc. Sew together the pieces.

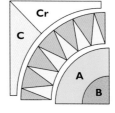

Block Assembly Diagram

4. Sew the neutral print C piece to the neutral print C reversed piece to make a C/C unit.

5. Pin the C/C unit to the outer edge of the pieced arc, matching the seam line of the C/C unit with the center mark on the pieced arc. Sew together the pieces to make a Crown of Thorns block. The pieced block should measure 7¼" square, including the seam allowances.

6. Repeat steps 1 through 5 to make a total of 48 Crown of Thorns blocks.

Assemble the Quilt Center

1. Referring to the photograph on *page 17* and the Quilt Assembly Diagram on *page 20*, lay out the pieced Crown of Thorns blocks, the bright blue sashing strips, and the solid red-orange sashing squares in sections.

2. Once you're pleased with the placement of the blocks, sew together the sections. Press the seam allowances open or toward the bright blue sashing strips. Then join the sections into rows. Sew together the rows to make the quilt center. The pieced quilt center should measure 44×58½", including the seam allowances.

Add the Inner Border

1. With midpoints aligned, sew the two bright blue print 1½×48" inner border strips to the top and bottom edges of the pieced quilt center and the two bright blue print 1½×63" inner border strips to the side edges of the pieced quilt center,

continued

Quilt Assembly Diagram

beginning and ending the seams ¼" from the corners.

2. Miter the corners. For information on mitering corners, see the instructions in Quilter's Schoolhouse, which begins on *page 145*. The pieced quilt center should now measure 46×60½", including the seam allowances.

Assemble and Add the Outer Border

1. Sew a blue or dark blue Asian print large triangle to opposite edges of a red Asian print 5½" square (see Diagram 5, left) to make a Unit 1. Press the seam allowances toward the blue print triangles. Repeat to make a total of four of Unit 1, then four of Unit 1 reversed (see Diagram 5, right).

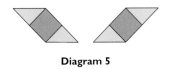

Diagram 5

2. Referring to Diagram 6, join a blue or dark blue Asian print large triangle and a blue or dark blue Asian print small triangle to opposite sides of a red Asian print 5½" square. Then add a second blue or dark blue Asian print small triangle to make a Unit 2. Press the seam allowances toward the blue print triangles. Repeat to make a second Unit 2.

Diagram 6   **Diagram 7**

3. Referring to Diagram 7, repeat Step 2, reversing the position of the blue print triangles to make a Unit 3. Press the seam allowances toward the blue print triangles. Repeat to make a second Unit 3.

4. Referring to Diagram 8 for placement, sew together two of Unit 1 reversed and one of Unit 3. Sew a gold Asian print 2½×27½" strip to the top edge of the pieced units. Trim the gold print strip even with the pieced units at both ends, making the angled end 45°. Mark and cut a 45° angle at one end of a red-and-blue Asian print 9⅝×46½" strip. Sew together the angled ends to make a side outer border unit. Trim the red-and-blue Asian print end so the side outer border unit measures 9⅝×62¼", including the seam allowances. Repeat to make a second side outer border unit.

Diagram 8

5. Sew a side outer border unit to each side edge of the pieced quilt top, aligning the red-and-blue Asian print end of the unit with the quilt top edge. There should be an excess 2¼" at the opposite edge.

6. Referring to Diagram 9, join two of Unit 1 and one of Unit 2. Sew a gold Asian print 2½×20½"

strip to the top edge of the pieced units, ending the strip 7⅛" from the straight edge of the pieced units as shown. Trim the gold print strip even with the 45° angled end of the pieced units. Mark and cut a 45° angle at one end of a red-and-blue Asian print 9⅝×46½" strip. Sew together the angled ends to make the top outer border unit. Trim the red-and-blue Asian print end so the top outer border unit measures 9⅝×64¼", including the seam allowances. Repeat to make a matching bottom outer border unit.

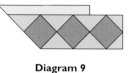

Diagram 9

7. Sew the top and bottom outer border units to the top and bottom edges of the pieced quilt center, beginning the seams ¼" from the corner of the gold strips and ending the seams at borders' edges.

8. Join the gold Asian print outer border strips with mitered corners, ending the seams ¼" from the outer border units (see Diagram 10). Sew together the remaining raw edges of the outer border units to complete the quilt top (see Diagram 11).

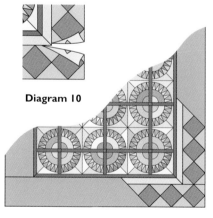

Diagram 10

Diagram 11

Complete the Quilt

1. Layer the quilt top, batting, and backing according to the instructions in Quilter's Schoolhouse, which begins on *page 145*. Quilt as desired.

2. Use the red-and-blue Asian print 2½×42" strips to bind the quilt according to the instructions in Quilter's Schoolhouse.

FRAMED SUNFLOWER

Piece together four blocks from the "Crown of Thorns" quilt without the sashing to create this picture-perfect work of art.

Materials

Scraps of assorted red, orange, and yellow prints for blocks

Scraps of assorted black prints for blocks and borders

Mat and frame

Finished project: 17½" square
Finished block: 6¾" square

continued

Cut the Fabrics

To make the best use of your fabrics, cut the pieces in the order that follows. The border strip measurements are mathematically correct. You may wish to cut your border strips longer than specified to allow for possible sewing differences.

This project uses "Crown of Thorns" patterns, which are on *Pattern Sheet 1*. Refer to the Trace the Foundation Papers instructions on *page 18* to make a total of four foundation-paper arcs.

From assorted red, orange, and yellow prints, cut:
- 4 of Pattern A
- 24—2¼×3" rectangles for foundation piecing

From assorted black prints, cut:
- 4 *each* of patterns B, C, and C reversed
- 28—2¼×3" rectangles for foundation piecing
- 2—1½×18" border strips
- 4—1½×16" border strips
- 2—1½×14" border strips

Assemble the Blocks

1. Referring to the Foundation-Piecing Method and Foundation-Piece the Arcs instructions on *pages 18 and 19*, use the assorted red, orange, yellow, and black print 2¼×3" rectangles to make a total of four pieced arcs.

2. Referring to Assemble the Crown of Thorns Blocks instructions on *page 19*, use one pieced arc, one red, orange, or yellow print A piece, one black print B piece, one black print C piece, and one black print C reversed piece to make a Crown of Thorns block. Repeat to make a total of four blocks.

Assemble the Quilt Center

Referring to the photograph on *page 21* for placement, lay out the blocks in two horizontal rows. Sew together the blocks in pairs. Press the seam allowances in opposite directions. Join the pairs to make the quilt center. The pieced quilt center should measure 14" square, including the seam allowances.

Add the Borders

1. Sew a black print 1½×14" border strip to the top and bottom edges of the pieced quilt center. Then add a black print 1½×16" border strip to each side edge of the pieced quilt center. Press all seam allowances toward the black print inner border.

2. Sew the remaining black print 1½×16" border strips to the top and bottom edges of the pieced quilt center. Then add a black print 1½×18" border strip to each side edge of the pieced quilt center to complete the quilt top. Press all seam allowances toward the outer black print border.

Complete the Quilt

Mat and frame as desired.

TABLETOP QUILT

Turning the points of each block toward the outer corners gives this variation on the "Crown of Thorns" quilt a different look.

Materials

⅛ yard of tone-on-tone plum print for blocks

⅛ yard of multicolor stripe for blocks

⅛ yard of tan print for blocks

⅛ yard of plum print for blocks

¼ yard of green print for blocks, border, and binding

⅛ yard of light tan print for border

½ yard of backing fabric

18" square of quilt batting

Finished quilt top: 15" square
Finished block: 6¾" square

Cut the Fabrics

To make the best use of your fabrics, cut the pieces in the order that follows. The border strip measurements are mathematically correct. You may wish to cut your border strips longer than specified to allow for possible sewing differences.

This project uses "Crown of Thorns" patterns, which are on *Pattern Sheet 1*. Refer to the Trace the Foundation Papers instructions on *page 18* to make a total of four foundation-paper arcs.

From tone-on-tone plum print, cut:
• 28—2¼×3" rectangles for foundation piecing

From multicolor stripe, cut:
• 24—2¼×3" rectangles for foundation piecing

From tan print, cut:
• 4 of Pattern A

From plum print, cut:
• 4 of Pattern B

From green print, cut:
• 4 *each* of patterns C and C reversed
• 2—2×42" binding strips
• 4—1¼" squares

From light tan print, cut:
• 4—1¼×13½" border strips

Assemble the Blocks

1. Referring to the Foundation-Piecing Method and Foundation-Piece the Arcs instructions on *pages 18 and 19*, use the tone-on-tone plum and multicolor stripe 2¼×3" rectangles to make a total of four pieced arcs.

2. Referring to Assemble the Crown of Thorns Blocks instructions on *page 19*, use one pieced arc, one tan print A piece, one plum print B piece, one green print C piece, and one green print C reversed piece to make a block. Repeat to make a total of four blocks.

Assemble the Quilt Center

1. Referring to the photograph *below* for placement, lay out the blocks in two horizontal rows. Sew

together the blocks in pairs. Press the seam allowances in opposite directions. Join the pairs to complete the quilt center. The pieced quilt center should measure 14" square, including the seam allowances.

2. Add a light tan print 1¼×13½" border strip to each side edge of the pieced quilt center. Press seam allowances toward the border. Join one green print 1¼" square to each end of the remaining tan print border strips. Sew the pieced border strips to the top and bottom edges of the pieced quilt center. Press the seam allowances toward the tan print border.

Complete the Quilt

1. Layer the quilt top, batting, and backing according to the instructions in Quilter's Schoolhouse, which begins on *page 145*. Quilt as desired.

2. Use the green print 2×42" strips to bind the quilt according to the instructions in Quilter's Schoolhouse.

Project designer Cleo Snuggerud collected

bits and pieces of pastel fabrics. Then she

stitched them into traditional Four-Patch blocks

and joined them with a pink-and-white

candy-cane-stripe sashing.

CANDY *Stripes*

Materials

2½ yards total of assorted florals, checks, stripes, and other prints for Four-Patch units

2¾ yards total of assorted light prints for Four-Patch units

3¼ yards of pink-and-white stripe for sashing and binding

5 yards of backing fabric

73×91" of quilt batting

Finished quilt top: 66¾×85"
Finished block: 3" square

Quantities specified for 44/45"-wide, 100% cotton fabrics. All measurements include a ¼" seam allowance. Sew with right sides together unless otherwise stated.

Select the Fabrics

Cleo Snuggerud, who designed the quilt and coordinating pillowcase shown *opposite*, recommends using as many soft pastel fabrics as you can find. She also says that randomly including a more vivid pastel in the Four-Patch blocks lends movement and vibrancy to the quilt.

Cut the Fabrics

To make the best use of your fabrics, cut the pieces in the order that follows.

continued

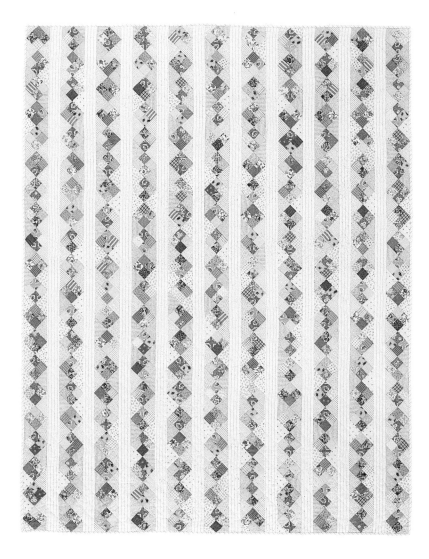

Cut the sashing strips the length of the fabric (parallel to the selvage). The measurements for the sashing strips are mathematically correct. You may wish to cut your sashing strips longer than specified to allow for possible sewing differences.

From assorted pastel florals, checks, stripes, and other prints, cut:
- 44—2×42" strips

From assorted light prints, cut:
- 116—5½" squares, cutting each in half diagonally twice in an X for a total of 464 triangles (there will be 2 left over)

From pink-and-white stripe, cut:
- 10—2½×85½" sashing strips
- 1—18×42" rectangle, cutting it into enough 2"-wide bias strips to total 310" in length (For specific cutting instructions, see Quilter's Schoolhouse, which begins on *page 145.*)

Assemble the Four-Patch Units

1. Aligning the long edges, sew together two assorted pastel 2×42" strips to make a strip set (see Diagram 1). Press the seam allowance in one direction. Cut the strip set into twenty 2"-wide segments.

Diagram 1

2. Repeat Step 1 to make a total of 22 strip sets and a total of 440 segments.

3. Sew together two 2"-wide segments to make a Four-Patch block (see Diagram 2). Press the seam allowance in one direction. The block should measure 3½" square, including the seam allowances. Repeat to make a total of 220 Four-Patch blocks.

Diagram 2

4. Join two assorted light print triangles to opposite edges of a Four-Patch block to make a Four-Patch unit (see Diagram 3). Press the seam allowances toward the light print triangles. Repeat to make a total of 220 Four-Patch units.

Diagram 3

Assemble the Rows

1. Referring to Diagram 4, join 20 Four-Patch units, carefully matching the seams, to make a row. Press the seam allowances in one direction.

2. Add a light print triangle to each end of the row. Square off the ends of the row, leaving a ¼" seam allowance (see Diagram 5). The pieced row should measure 4¾×85½", including the seam allowances.

3. Repeat steps 1 and 2 to make a total of 11 pieced rows.

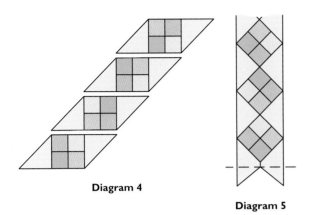

Diagram 4

Diagram 5

4. Referring to the photograph *opposite*, lay out the 11 pieced rows and 10 pink-and-white stripe 2½×85½" sashing strips in alternating rows.

5. Sew together the rows to complete the quilt top. Press the seam allowances toward the sashing strips.

Complete the Quilt

1. Layer the quilt top, batting, and backing according to the instructions in Quilter's Schoolhouse, which begins on *page 145*. Quilt as desired.

2. Use the pink-and-white stripe 2"-wide bias strips to bind the quilt according to the instructions in Quilter's Schoolhouse.

PILLOWCASE

Complete the ensemble with coordinating

pillowcases accented with bands of

Four-Patch blocks.

Materials to make one standard-size pillowcase

1¼ yards pink-and-white stripe for pillowcase and sashing

⅛ yard total of assorted pastel florals, checks, stripes, and other prints for Four-Patch units

¼ yard total of assorted light prints for Four-Patch units

Cut the Fabrics

To make the best use of your fabrics, cut the pieces in the order that follows. Cut the pink-and-white stripe pieces the length of the fabric (parallel to the selvage).

continued

Candy Stripes Quilt
optional sizes

If you'd like to make this quilt in a size other than for a twin bed, use the information *below*.

Alternate quilt sizes	Crib/Lap	Full/Queen	King
Number of blocks	91	322	459
Number of blocks wide by long	7×13	14×23	17×27
Sashing strips	6	13	16
Finished size	41¾×55¼"	85½×97¾"	104¼×114¾"
Yardage requirements			
Total of assorted pastel florals, checks, stripes, and prints	1¼ yards	3½ yards	5 yards
Total of assorted light prints	1¼ yards	4 yards	5½ yards
Pink-and-white stripe	1¾ yards	3⅝ yards	4¼ yards
Backing	2⅔ yards	7⅔ yards	9¼ yards
Batting	60" square	96×108"	120" square

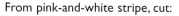

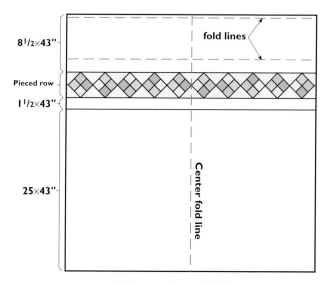

Pillowcase Assembly Diagram

From pink-and-white stripe, cut:
- 1—25×43" rectangle
- 1—8½×43" strip
- 1—1½×43" strip

From assorted pastel florals, checks, stripes, and other prints, cut:
- 40—2" squares

From assorted light prints, cut:
- 6—5½" squares, cutting each in half diagonally twice in an X for a total of 24 triangles (there will be 2 left over)

Assemble the Four-Patch Band

1. Referring to Diagram 2 on *page 26*, lay out four assorted pastel print 2" squares. Sew together the squares in rows, then join the rows to make a Four-Patch block. The Four-Patch block should measure 3½" square. Repeat to make a total of 10 Four-Patch blocks.

2. Referring to Assemble the Four-Patch Units, Step 4, on *page 26*, make a total of 10 Four-Patch units.

3. Referring to the Assemble the Rows instructions beginning on *page 26*, use the 10 units and two triangles to make one row. The pieced row should measure 4¾×43", including the seam allowances.

Assemble the Pillowcase

1. Lay out the pieces for the pillowcase, referring to the Pillowcase Assembly Diagram for placement. Sew together the pieces, pressing the seams away from the Four-Patch band.

2. Fold the pillowcase unit in half along the center fold line and sew together the long edges and the short edges farthest from the pieced row. Press the seam allowances to one side. Turn the pillowcase right side out.

3. Fold the unfinished edge under ½" and press. Then fold it under 6½", leaving a 1"-wide strip along the pieced row. Topstitch the folded section in place.

JUNGLE WALL HANGING

The "Candy Stripes" pattern marches to a different beat as a jungle-inspired border print runs between rows of the familiar Four-Patch units.

Materials

Scraps of assorted jungle, animal, stripe, and other prints for Four-Patch units

¼ yard of solid black for Four-Patch units

⅔ yard of jungle border print for sashing

⅛ yard of black-and-gold stripe for inner border

½ yard of geometric print for outer border

¼ yard of black-and-white print for binding

⅞ yard of backing fabric

34×31" of quilt batting

Cherished Classics

Finished quilt top: 28¾×25¾"
Finished block: 3" square

Cut the Fabrics

To make the best use of your fabrics, cut the pieces in the order that follows. The border strip measurements are mathematically correct. You may wish to cut your border strips longer than specified to allow for possible sewing differences.

From assorted jungle, animal, stripe, and other prints, cut:

- 40—2" squares

From solid black, cut:

- 6—5½" squares, cutting each in half diagonally twice in an X for a total of 24 triangles

From jungle border print, cut:

- 2—3⅞×21¾" sashing strips
- 1—3½×21¾" sashing strip

From black-and-gold stripe, cut:

- 2—1¼×21¾" inner border strips
- 2—1¼×20¼" inner border strips

From geometric print, cut:

- 2—3½×26¼" outer border strips
- 2—3½×23¼" outer border strips

From black-and-white print, cut:

- 3—2½×42" binding strips

Assemble the Four-Patch Units

1. Referring to the Assemble the Four-Patch Units instructions on *page 26*, use the assorted print 2" squares and 20 solid black triangles to make a total of 10 Four-Patch units.

2. Referring to the Assemble the Rows instructions on *page 26*, join five Four-Patch units and two solid black triangles into a row. The pieced row should measure 4¾×21¾", including the seam allowances. Repeat to make a second pieced row.

Assemble the Quilt Center

1. Referring to the photograph *above*, lay out the two 4¾×21¾" pieced rows, the two jungle border print 3⅞×21¾" sashing strips, and the one jungle border print 3½×21¾" sashing strip; join to make the quilt center. Press the seam allowances toward the sashing strips. The pieced quilt center should measure 21¾×18¾", including seam allowances.

2. Join a black-and-gold stripe 1¼×21¾" inner border strip to the top and bottom edges of the pieced

quilt center. Then add a black-and-gold stripe 1¼×20¼" inner border strip to each side edge of the pieced quilt center. Press all seam allowances toward the inner border.

3. Sew a geometric print 3½×23¼" outer border strip to the top and bottom edges of the pieced quilt center. Then sew a geometric print 3½×26¼" outer border strip to each side edge of the pieced quilt center to complete the quilt top. Press all seam allowances toward the outer border.

Complete the Quilt

1. Layer the quilt top, batting, and backing according to the instructions in Quilter's Schoolhouse, which begins on *page 145*.

2. Quilt as desired. This wall quilt was machine-quilted in the ditch along the sashing and just outside each Four-Patch block. The animals in the sashing were outline-quilted. The black triangles of the Four-Patch units were stipple-quilted and the border was quilted along the strong diagonal print lines.

3. Use the black-and-white print 2½×42" binding strips to bind the quilt according to the instructions in Quilter's Schoolhouse.

SIMPLE
SENSATIONS

Quilters have long appreciated uncomplicated

projects. In fact, quiltmakers have often memorized

easy patterns that best featured the fabrics they

had available to them. Current quilters who are

no different will like these versatile, rotary-cut

designs that can incorporate a variety of fabrics.

These projects work well as quick-to-make gifts and

home-decorating accessories.

The use of plaid and stripe fabric in quiltmaking is enjoying a resurgence in popularity. Much of the charm of antique scrap quilts was a result of these fabrics. Old clothing provided the early quiltmaker with a variety of choices. Little did she know that years later we would have to work at achieving this same look in our quilts.

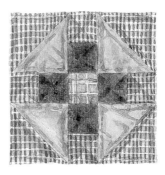

Checkmate

Materials

2 yards of solid black for blocks and setting triangles

1¾ yards total of assorted checks and plaids for blocks and inner border

1⅛ yards total of assorted solid colors for blocks

1¾ yards of solid tan for outer border and binding

3½ yards of backing fabric

61×72" of quilt batting

Finished quilt top: 55½×66⅛"
Finished block: 7½" square

Quantities specified for 44/45"-wide, 100% cotton fabrics. All measurements include a ¼" seam allowance. Sew with right sides together unless otherwise stated.

Cut the Fabrics

To make the best use of your fabrics, cut the pieces in the order that follows.

Cut the border strips the length of the fabric (parallel to the selvage). The border strip measurements are mathematically correct. You may wish to cut your border strips longer than specified to allow for possible sewing differences.

continued

From solid black, cut:

- 4—12" squares, cutting each diagonally twice in an X for a total of 16 side triangles (there will be 2 left over)
- 2—6¼" squares, cutting each in half diagonally for a total of 4 corner triangles
- 40—3⅞" squares, cutting each in half diagonally for a total of 80 small triangles
- 32—2×10" strips

From assorted checks and plaids, cut:

- 24—3⅞" squares, cutting each in half diagonally for a total of 48 small triangles (To get 12 sets of 4 matching triangles, as was done here, cut squares in sets of 2.)
- 32—2×10" strips
- 32—2" squares

From assorted solid colors, cut:

- 64—3⅞" squares, cutting each in half diagonally for a total of 128 small triangles (To get 32 sets of 4 matching triangles, as was done here, cut squares in sets of 2.)

From solid tan, cut:

- 2—5½×56⅝" outer border strips
- 2—5½×56" outer border strips
- 6—2½×42" binding strips

Assemble Block A

1. Aligning long edges, sew together one solid black 2×10" strip and one check or plaid 2×10" strip to make a strip set (see Diagram 1). Press the seam allowance toward the solid black strip. Cut the strip set into four 2"-wide segments.

Diagram 1   **Diagram 2**

2. Aligning long edges, sew together one solid black small triangle and one solid-color small triangle to make a triangle-square (see Diagram 2). Press the seam allowance toward the solid black triangle. Repeat to make a total of four matching triangle-squares.

3. Referring to the Block A Assembly Diagram, lay out the four 2"-wide segments from Step 1, the four triangle-squares from Step 2, and one check or plaid 2" square in three horizontal rows. Join the pieces in each row. Press the seam allowances in one direction, alternating directions with each

row. Then join the rows to make a Block A. Pieced Block A should measure 8" square, including the seam allowances.

4. Repeat steps 1 through 3 to make a total of 20 of Block A.

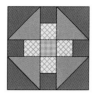

Block A   **Block B**
Assembly Diagram   **Assembly Diagram**

Assemble Block B

1. Repeat Step 1 under Assemble Block A to make a strip set and four 2"-wide segments.

2. Aligning long edges, sew together one solid-color small triangle and one check or plaid triangle to make a triangle-square. Press the seam allowance toward the solid-color triangle. Repeat to make a total of four matching triangle-squares.

3. Referring to the Block B Assembly Diagram, lay out the four 2"-wide segments from Step 1, the four triangle-squares from Step 2, and one check or plaid 2" square in three horizontal rows. Join the pieces in each row. Press the seam allowances in one direction, alternating directions with each row. Then join the rows to make a Block B. Pieced Block B should measure 8" square, including the seam allowances.

4. Repeat steps 1 through 3 to make a total of 12 of Block B.

Assemble the Quilt Center

1. Referring to the Quilt Assembly Diagram for placement, lay out the 32 pieced blocks A and B, 14 solid black side triangles, and the four solid black corner triangles in eight diagonal rows. Sew together the pieces in each row, except for the corner triangles. Press the seam allowances in one direction, alternating the direction with each row.

2. Join the rows, adding the corner triangles last, to complete the quilt center. The pieced quilt center should measure 43×53⅝", including the seam allowances.

Cut, Assemble, and Add the Inner Border

1. From the remaining check and plaid scraps, cut 2"-wide strips of various lengths. Sew together the strips end to end to make the following:
   - 2—2×53⅝" inner border strips
   - 2—2×46" inner border strips

2. Sew a long inner border strip to each side edge of the pieced quilt center. Then add a short inner border strip to the top and bottom edges of the pieced quilt center. Press all seam allowances toward the inner border.

Add the Outer Border

Sew one solid tan 5½×56⅝" outer border strip to each side edge of the pieced quilt center. Then add one solid tan 5½×56" outer border strip to the top and bottom edges of the pieced quilt center to complete the quilt top. Press the seam allowances toward the outer border.

Complete the Quilt

1. Layer the quilt top, batting, and backing according to the instructions in Quilter's Schoolhouse, which begins on *page 145*. Quilt as desired.

2. Use the solid tan 2½×42" strips to bind the quilt according to the instructions in Quilter's Schoolhouse.

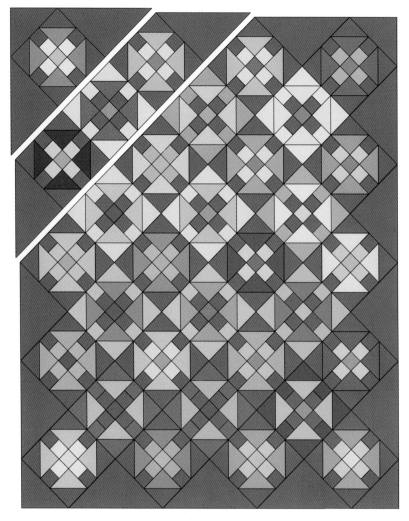

Quilt Assembly Diagram

Checkmate Quilt
optional sizes

If you'd like to make this quilt in a size other than for a wall hanging, use the information *below*.

Alternate quilt sizes	Crib/Lap	Full/Queen	King
Number of Block A	12	56	81
Number of Block B	6	42	64
Number of blocks wide by long	3×4	7×8	9×9
Finished size	44⅞×55½"	87⅜×98"	108⅝" square
Yardage requirements			
Solid black	1½ yards	4 yards	5⅛ yards
Assorted checks and plaids	1⅛ yards	3½ yards	8½ yards
Assorted solid colors	⅝ yard	2½ yards	3½ yards
Solid tan	1½ yards	2¾ yards	3¼ yards
Backing	2⅞ yards	7⅞ yards	9⅝ yards
Batting	51×62"	94×104"	115" square

Simple Sensations

DUVET COVER

Want to liven up a room in a hurry?

This duvet cover—with its big blocks and

turned-down edge—makes a wonderful

weekend project.

Materials

7 yards total of assorted bright prints for blocks

½ yard of mottled green print for blocks

2⅜ yards of lilac polka dot for borders

4⅞ yards of multicolor bright print for backing fabric

Hook-and-loop tape fastener tabs

Finished duvet cover: 82½×97½"
  (fits a full/queen-size comforter)
Finished block: 7½" square

Cut the Fabrics

To make the best use of your fabrics, cut the pieces in the order that follows.

Cut the border strips the length of the fabric (parallel to the selvage). The border strip measurements are mathematically correct. You may wish to cut your border strips longer than specified to allow for possible sewing differences.

From assorted bright prints, cut:
• 20—8⅜" squares, cutting each in half diagonally for a total of 40 large triangles
• 123—8" squares
• 18—3⅞" squares, cutting each in half diagonally for a total of 36 small triangles
• 9—2×10" strips
• 9—2" squares

From mottled green print, cut:
• 2—8" squares
• 18—3⅞" squares, cutting each in half diagonally for a total of 36 small triangles
• 9—2×10" strips

From lilac polka dot, cut:
• 1—4¼×83" strip
• 1—8×83" strip

From multicolor bright print, cut and piece:
• 1—83×96" rectangle for backing

Assemble the Triangle-Squares

Referring to Diagram 2 on *page 34*, sew together two bright print large triangles to make a triangle-square. Press the seam allowance in one direction. The pieced triangle-square should measure 8" square, including the seam allowances. Repeat to make a total of 20 triangle-squares.

Assemble the Duvet Top

1. Referring to the photograph at *right* for placement, lay out the 20 triangle-squares and the 123 bright print 8" squares in 13 horizontal rows.

2. Sew together the blocks in each row, pressing the seam allowances to one side and alternating the direction with each row. Then join the rows to make the duvet top. Press the seam allowances in one direction. The pieced duvet top should measure 83×98", including the seam allowances.

Assemble Block A

Referring to the Assemble Block A instructions on *page 34*, use one bright print 2×10" strip, one mottled green print 2×10" strip, four bright print small triangles, four mottled green print small triangles, and one bright print 2" square to make a Block A. Repeat to make a total of five of Block A.

Assemble Block B

Referring to the Assemble Block B instructions on *page 34*, use one bright print 2×10" strip, one mottled green print 2×10" strip, four bright print small triangles, four mottled green print small triangles, and one bright print 2" square to make a Block B. Repeat to make a total of four of Block B.

Assemble the Duvet Cover

1. Referring to the photograph at *right* for placement, lay out the nine pieced blocks A and B and the two mottled green print 8" squares in a horizontal row. Sew together the blocks. The patchwork row should measure 8×83", including the seam allowances.

2. Sew the lilac polka dot 4¼×83" strip to one long edge of the patchwork row. Then join the lilac polka dot 8×83" strip to the remaining long edge. Press the seam allowances toward the strips.

3. Turn the raw edge of the 8"-wide lilac polka dot strip under ¼" and press. Then fold it under 3¾",

Duvet Top

The back border is not sewn to the backing fabric along this edge. This creates the envelope-style opening through which you insert the comforter.

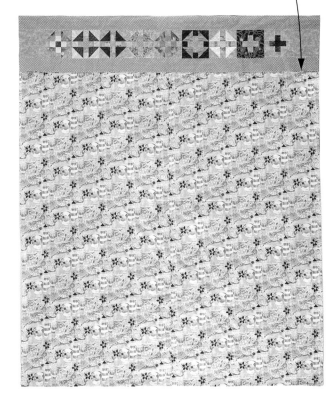

Duvet Back

continued

creating a hem. Topstitch the folded hem in place to complete the back border.

4. Sew hook-and-loop tape tabs at even intervals along the hemmed edge of the back border.

5. Turn under ¼" along a short edge of the backing 83×96" rectangle; press. Then fold under 3¾", creating a hem. Topstitch the hem in place.

6. Pin the raw edge of the back border to the top edge of the duvet front. Then add the hemmed duvet backing, aligning the bottom edge with the duvet front; the upper edge will overlap the back border (see Diagram 1). Sew together around all the outside edges to create the duvet cover (see Diagram 2). Do not sew across the bottom hemmed edge of the back border. Turn the duvet cover right side out and press. The border will lap over the backing to form an envelope.

7. Sew reciprocal hook-and-loop tape tabs along the backing hemmed edge to align with those on the back border. Insert a comforter through the envelope-style opening and latch the hook-and-loop tape tabs to secure.

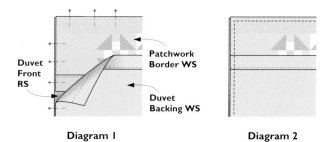

Diagram I   Diagram 2

WALL QUILT

This quilt will add pizzazz to your room, whether you hang it on the wall or toss it over a comfy chair.

Finished quilt top: 55½×66⅛"
Finished block: 7½" square

Cut the Fabrics

To make the best use of your fabrics, cut the pieces in the order that follows.

Cut the border strips the length of the fabric (parallel to the selvage). Extra length has been added to allow for mitered corners. You may wish to cut your border strips longer than specified to allow for possible sewing differences.

From green print, cut:
- 4—12" squares, cutting each diagonally twice in an X for a total of 16 side triangles (there will be 2 left over)
- 2—6¼" squares, cutting each in half diagonally for a total of 4 corner triangles
- 64—3⅞" squares, cutting each in half diagonally for a total of 128 small triangles
- 32—2×10" strips

Simple Sensations

From assorted bright prints, cut:

- 64—3⅞" squares, cutting each in half diagonally for a total of 128 small triangles (To get 32 sets of 4 matching triangles, as was done here, cut squares in sets of 2.)
- 32—2×10" strips
- 32—2" squares

From multicolor stripe, cut:

- 2—5½×68⅝" outer border strips
- 2—5½×58" outer border strips

From lilac polka dot, cut:

- 7—2½×42" binding strips

Assemble Block A

Referring to the Assemble Block A instructions on *page 34*, use one bright print 2×10" strip, one green print 2×10" strip, four bright print small triangles, four green print small triangles, and one bright print 2" square to make a Block A. Repeat to make a total of 20 of Block A.

Assemble Block B

Referring to the Assemble Block B instructions on *page 34*, use one bright print 2×10" strip, one green print 2×10" strip, four bright print small triangles, four green print small triangles, and one bright print 2" square to make a Block B. Repeat to make a total of 12 of Block B.

Assemble the Quilt Center

Referring to the photograph *right* for placement, lay out the 32 pieced blocks A and B, the 14 green print side triangles, and the four green print corner triangles in eight diagonal rows. Referring to the Assemble the Quilt Center instructions on *page 34*, sew together the quilt center. The pieced quilt center should measure 43×53⅝", including the seam allowances.

Cut, Assemble, and Add the Inner Border

From the remaining bright print scraps, cut 2"-wide strips of various lengths. Sew together the strips end to end to make the following:

- 2—2×53⅝" inner border strips
- 2—2×46" inner border strips

Referring to the Cut, Assemble, and Add the Inner Border instructions on *page 35*, Step 2, join the inner border to the pieced quilt center. The pieced quilt center should now measure 46×56⅝".

Add the Outer Border

1. With midpoints aligned, sew the two multicolor stripe 5½×68⅝" outer border strips to the side edges of the pieced quilt center and the two multicolor stripe 5½×58" outer border strips to the top and bottom edges of the pieced quilt center, beginning and ending the seams ¼" from the corners.

2. Miter the corners. For information on mitering corners, see the instructions in Quilter's Schoolhouse, which begins on *page 145*.

Complete the Quilt

1. Layer the quilt top, batting, and backing according to the instructions in Quilter's Schoolhouse. Quilt as desired.

2. Use the lilac polka dot 2½×42" strips to bind the quilt according to the instructions in Quilter's Schoolhouse.

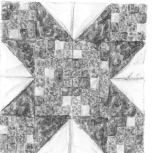

ENGLISH
Trellis

Rotary cutting and strip piecing speed up the creation of the 64-patch units

central to this project. When they are stitched together with triangle-squares and

16-patch units, the resulting pattern resembles a garden trellis.

Materials

¾ yard of tan-and-pink print (color No. 1) for blocks

½ yard of tan tone-on-tone print (color No. 2) for blocks

¾ yard of green print (color No. 3) for blocks

¾ yard of pink print (color No. 4) for blocks

½ yard of tan print (color No. 5) for blocks

1⅛ yards of solid ecru for blocks

2⅛ yards of green tone-on-tone print for blocks and inner border

3⅛ yards of tan floral print for outer border and binding

4⅞ yards of backing fabric

76×88" of quilt batting

Finished quilt top: 70×82"
Finished block: 12" square

Quantities specified for 44/45"-wide, 100% cotton fabrics. All measurements include a ¼" seam allowance. Sew with right sides together unless otherwise stated.

continued

Cut the Fabrics

To make the best use of your fabrics, cut the pieces in the order that follows.

Cut the border strips the length of the fabric (parallel to the selvage). The border strips' extra length allows for mitering the corners.

From tan-and-pink print, cut:
- 20—1¼×42" strips

From tan tone-on-tone print, cut:
- 10—1¼×42" strips

From green print, cut:
- 20—1¼×42" strips

From pink print, cut:
- 20—1¼×42" strips

From tan print, cut:
- 10—1¼×42" strips

From solid ecru, cut:
- 80—3⅞" squares, cutting each in half diagonally to make 160 triangles

From green tone-on-tone print, cut:
- 2—3½×70½" inner border strips
- 2—3½×58½" inner border strips
- 80—3⅞" squares, cutting each in half diagonally to make 160 triangles

From tan floral print, cut:
- 2—8½×90½" outer border strips
- 2—8½×78½" outer border strips
- 8—2½×42" binding strips

Assemble the Star Blocks

1. Sew together one tan-and-pink print 1¼×42" strip, one tan tone-on-tone print 1¼×42" strip, one green print 1¼×42" strip, and one pink print 1¼×42" strip to make a strip set (see Diagram 1). Press the seam allowances toward the tan-and-pink print strip. Repeat to make a total of 10 strip sets.

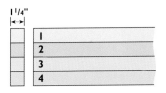

Diagram 1

2. Cut each strip set into thirty-two 1¼"-wide segments for a total of 320 segments.

3. Sew together one tan print 1¼×42" strip, one tan-and-pink print 1¼×42" strip, one pink print 1¼×42" strip, and one green print 1¼×42" strip to make a strip set (see Diagram 2). Press the seam allowances toward the green print strip. Repeat to make a total of 10 strip sets.

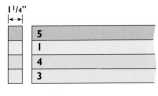

Diagram 2

4. Cut each strip set into thirty-two 1¼"-wide segments for a total of 320 segments.

5. Sew together two 1¼"-wide segments from Step 2 (reversing one) and two 1¼"-wide segments from Step 4 (reversing one) to make a 16-patch unit (see Diagram 3). Press the seam allowances in one direction. The pieced 16-patch unit should measure 3½" square, including the seam allowances. Repeat to make a total of 160 of the 16-patch units.

1	2r	2	1r
1	5	3	4
2	1	4	3
3	4	1	2
4	3	5	1

Diagram 3

6. Sew together four 16-patch units to make a 64-patch unit (see Diagram 4). Press the seam allowances in one direction. The pieced 64-patch unit should measure 6½" square, including the seam allowances. Repeat to make a total of 20 of the 64-patch units.

4	3	2	1	1	5	3	4
3	4	1	5	2	1	4	3
5	1	4	3	3	4	1	2
1	2	3	4	4	3	5	1
1	5	3	4	4	3	2	1
2	1	4	3	3	4	1	5
3	4	1	2	5	1	4	3
4	3	5	1	1	2	3	4

Diagram 4

7. Sew together one solid ecru triangle and one green tone-on-tone print triangle to make a triangle-square (see Diagram 5). Press the seam allowance toward the green tone-on-tone print triangle. The pieced triangle-square should measure 3½" square, including the seam allowances. Repeat to make a total of 160 triangle-squares.

Diagram 5

8. Referring to Diagram 6, lay out one 64-patch unit, four 16-patch units, and eight triangle-squares in three rows. Sew together the squares in each row. Press the seam allowances toward the triangle-squares. Then join the rows to make a star block. Press the seam allowances in one direction. The pieced star block should measure 12½" square, including the seam allowances. Repeat to make a total of 20 star blocks.

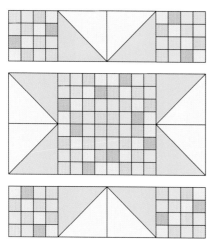

Diagram 6

Assemble the Quilt Center

I. Referring to the photograph *above right,* lay out the pieced star blocks in five horizontal rows.

2. Sew together the blocks in each row. Press the seam allowances in one direction, alternating the direction with each row. Join the rows to make the quilt center. The pieced quilt center should measure 48½×60½", including the seam allowances.

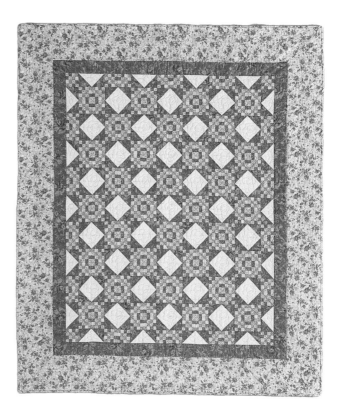

Assemble and Add the Borders

I. With midpoints aligned, join one green tone-on-tone print 3½×70½" inner border strip and one tan floral print 8½×90½" outer border strip to make a side border strip set. Repeat to make a second side border strip set. In the same manner, join one green tone-on-tone print 3½×58½" inner border strip and one tan floral print 8½×78½" outer border strip to make a top border strip set. Repeat to make a bottom border strip set.

2. With midpoints aligned and mitering the corners, add the long border strip sets to the side edges of the pieced quilt center and the short border strip sets to the top and bottom edges of the pieced quilt center to complete the quilt top. For information on mitering, see the instructions in Quilter's Schoolhouse, which begins on *page 145*.

Complete the Quilt

I. Layer the quilt top, batting, and backing according to the instructions in Quilter's Schoolhouse. Quilt as desired.

2. Use the tan floral print 2½×42" strips to bind the quilt according to the instructions in Quilter's Schoolhouse.

English Trellis

continued

English Trellis Quilt
optional sizes

If you'd like to make the quilt in a size other than what is given, use the information *below*.

Alternate quilt sizes	Crib/Lap	Full/Queen	King
Number of blocks	6	30	42
Number of blocks wide by long	2×3	5×6	6×7
Finished size	46×58"	82×94"	94×106"
Yardage requirements			
Tan-and-pink print (color No. 1) for blocks	¼ yard	1⅛ yards	1½ yards
Tan tone-on-tone print (color No. 2) for blocks	⅛ yard	⅝ yard	⅞ yard
Green print (color No. 3) for blocks	¼ yard	1⅛ yards	1½ yards
Pink print (color No. 4) for blocks	¼ yard	1⅛ yards	1½ yards
Tan print (color No. 5) for blocks	⅛ yard	⅝ yard	⅞ yard
Solid ecru for blocks	½ yard	1½ yards	2⅛ yards
Green tone-on-tone for blocks and inner border	1½ yards	2½ yards	2¾ yards
Tan floral print for outer border and binding	2½ yards	3⅝ yards	4¼ yards
Backing	2⅞ yards	7⅓ yards	8⅓ yards
Batting	52×64"	88×100"	100×112"

BATIK QUILT

Spectacular batik fabrics combined into triangle-squares result in this dynamic, contemporary quilt. Careful color placement and rotation of the triangle-squares as they're sewn into blocks create the repetitive pattern.

Materials

4⅓ yards of pink-and-purple batik print for blocks, border, and binding

2½ yards total of assorted teal, blue, and purple batik prints for blocks

4⅛ yards of backing fabric

74" square of quilt batting

Finished quilt top: 68" square
Finished block: 6" square

Cut the Fabrics

To make the best use of your fabrics, cut the pieces in the order that follows.

The border strip measurements are mathematically correct. You may wish to cut your border strips longer than specified to allow for possible sewing differences.

From pink-and-purple batik print, cut:
- 200—3⅞" squares, cutting each in half diagonally for a total of 400 triangles
- 8—2½" squares
- 8—4½×42" strips for border
- 7—2½×42" binding strips

From assorted teal, blue, and purple batik prints, cut:
- 200—3⅞" squares, cutting each in half diagonally for a total of 400 triangles
- 4—2½×4½" rectangles

Assemble the Blocks

1. Referring to Diagram 5 on *page 43*, join one pink-and-purple batik print triangle and one teal, blue, or purple batik print triangle to make a triangle-square. The triangle-square should measure 3½" square, including the seam allowances. Repeat to make a total of 400 triangle-squares.

2. Referring to Diagram 1, lay out four triangle-squares in two rows. Sew together the squares in pairs. Press the seam allowances in opposite directions; then join the pairs to make a Block A. Press the seam allowance to one side. Pieced Block A should measure 6½" square, including the seam allowances. Repeat to make a total of 50 of Block A.

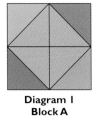

Diagram 1
Block A

3. Referring to Diagram 2, lay out four triangle-squares in two rows. Sew together the squares in pairs. Press the seam allowances in opposite directions; then join the pairs to make a Block B. Press the seam allowance to one side. Pieced Block B should measure 6½" square, including the seam allowances. Repeat to make a total of 50 of Block B.

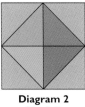

Diagram 2
Block B

Assemble the Quilt Center

Referring to the photograph on *page 46*, lay out the blocks in 10 horizontal rows, alternating Block A and Block B. Sew together the blocks in each row. Press the seam allowances toward the B blocks. Then join the rows to complete the quilt center. The pieced quilt center should measure 60½" square, including the seam allowances.

Assemble and Add the Borders

1. For accurate sewing lines, use a quilting pencil to mark each pink-and-purple batik print 2½" square with a diagonal line on the wrong side of the fabric. (To prevent your fabric from stretching as you draw the lines, place 220-grit sandpaper under the squares.)

2. Align one marked pink-and-purple batik print square with one end of a teal, blue, or purple batik print 2½×4½" rectangle

continued

including the seam allowances. Repeat to make a total of four Flying Geese units.

Diagram 4

4. Sew one 4½×42" pink-and-purple batik print strip to each long edge of a Flying Geese unit. Press the seam allowances toward the strips to make a pieced border unit. Repeat to make a total of four pieced border units.

5. With the tip of each border unit's Flying Geese unit pointing to the right, measure and mark 10" below the base of the Flying Geese unit. Aligning the marks with the centers of the side edges, add the pieced border units to the edges of the pieced quilt center, mitering the corners, to complete the quilt top. For information on mitering, see the instructions in Quilter's Schoolhouse, which begins on *page 145*.

Complete the Quilt

1. Layer the quilt top, batting, and backing according to the instructions in Quilter's Schoolhouse.

2. Quilt as desired. This project was machine-quilted. It has a swirling design in the center of the quilt, with geometric lines surrounding the swirl; the border was stippled.

3. Use the pink-and-purple batik print 2½×42" strips to bind the quilt according to the instructions in Quilter's Schoolhouse.

(see Diagram 3, note the placement of the marked line). Stitch on the marked line. Trim the seam allowance to ¼". Press open the attached pink-and-purple print batik triangle.

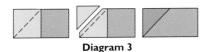

Diagram 3

3. In the same manner, sew a second marked pink-and-purple batik print square on the opposite end of the same rectangle; trim and press open to make a Flying Geese unit (see Diagram 4). The Flying Geese unit should still measure 2½×4½",

CHECKERBOARD

With its no-fray finish, felted wool is the perfect fabric choice to create this folk art game board. Simple blanket stitching enhances the charm of the game board and checkers.

Materials

⅛ yard *each* of solid lilac, green, pink, and gold felted wool for appliqués

11" square of cotton print for backing

Embroidery floss: lilac, green, pink, and gold

Finished checkerboard top: 12½" square

Designer Notes

This project uses felted wool, which allows for crisp, clean-cut edges that don't need to be turned under and will not ravel.

To felt wool, machine-wash it in a hot-water wash/cool rinse cycle with a small amount of detergent, machine-dry, and steam-press.

Cut the Fabrics

To make the best use of your fabrics, cut the pieces in the order that follows. The patterns for this project are on *Pattern Sheet 2*. To make templates of the patterns, follow the instructions in Quilter's Schoolhouse, which begins on *page 145*.

From solid lilac felted wool, cut:
- 32—1¼" squares
- 4 of Pattern A

From solid green felted wool, cut:
- 32—1¼" squares
- 4 of Pattern A

From solid pink felted wool, cut:
- 12 of Pattern B
- 4 of Pattern A

From solid gold felted wool, cut:
- 12 of Pattern B
- 4 of Pattern A

Appliqué the Checkerboard

1. Turn under the edges of the 11" square of cotton print backing fabric ½" and baste in place.

2. Referring to the photograph *above right* for placement, arrange the 32 lilac 1¼" squares and the 32 green 1¼" squares in eight rows on the cotton print backing fabric, alternating lilac and green. Pin or baste the pieces in place.

3. Working from the center outward and using two strands of contrasting embroidery floss, blanket-stitch around the edges of each square, securing them to the backing fabric; leave the first and last squares in each row unstitched.

To blanket-stitch, first pull the needle up at A (see diagram *above right*). Form a reverse L shape with the floss, and hold the angle of the L shape in place with your thumb. Push the needle down at B and come up at C to secure the stitch. Repeat until you've stitched around the shape.

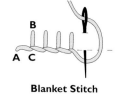

Blanket Stitch

4. Using two strands of contrasting embroidery floss, blanket-stitch around the curved edge of each A piece.

5. Referring to the photograph, arrange and pin the 16 A pieces around the perimeter of the checkerboard, inserting their flat edges between the unsewn squares and backing fabric.

6. Blanket-stitch around the edges of the remaining squares, securing the A pieces in place. Slip-stitch the edges of the backing fabric in place to complete the checkerboard.

7. Using two strands of contrasting embroidery floss, blanket-stitch around the edge of each pink and gold B circle to make the game pieces.

The sturdy work shirts of loggers inspired the fabric choices in this

robust quilt. At first glance, the pattern may seem random and complicated,

but both the Windblown Star and the alternate block are assembled

from easy-to-cut triangles.

Lumberjack

Simple Sensations

Materials

2¼ yards of black check for blocks

1⅜ yards of red print No. 1 for blocks

1¼ yards of red-and-black check for alternate blocks
    and border corners

1¼ yards of black print for inner border and binding

1½ yards of red print No. 2 for outer border

4⅔ yards of backing fabric

84" square of quilt batting

Finished quilt top: 78" square
Finished block: 12" square

Quantities specified for 44/45"-wide, 100% cotton fabrics. All measurements include a ¼" seam allowance. Sew with right sides together unless otherwise stated.

continued

Cut the Fabrics

To make the best use of your fabrics, cut the pieces in the order listed in each section.

Cut and Assemble the Windblown Star Blocks

From black check, cut:
- 11—3⅞×42" strips

From red print No. 1, cut:
- 11—3⅞×42" strips

1. Layer the black check and red print 3⅞×42" strips in pairs. Press the layered strips together to keep them from shifting while cutting.

2. From layered strips, cut:
   - 104—3⅞" squares, cutting each in half diagonally for a total of 208 triangle pairs

3. Sew together a layered triangle pair along the longest edges (see Diagram 1), being careful not to stretch the edges out of shape. Press open, pressing the seam allowance toward the red print triangle, to make a triangle-square (see Diagram 2). The triangle-square should measure 3½" square, including the seam allowances. Repeat to make a total of 208 triangle-squares.

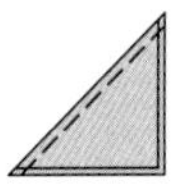

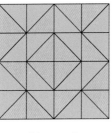

Diagram 1 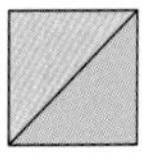   **Diagram 2**

4. Referring to Diagram 3 for placement, lay out four horizontal rows of four triangle-squares each.

Diagram 3

5. Sew together the triangle-squares in each row. Press the seam allowances in one direction, alternating the direction with each row. Then join the rows to make a Windblown Star block. Press the seam allowances in one direction. The pieced

Windblown Star block should measure 12½" square, including the seam allowances.

6. Repeat steps 4 and 5 to make a total of 13 Windblown Star blocks.

Cut and Assemble the Alternate Blocks

From black check, cut:
- 2—13¼×42" strips

From red-and-black check, cut:
- 2—13¼×42" strips

1. Layer the black check and red-and-black check strips in pairs. Press the layered strips together.

2. From the layered strips, cut:
   - 6—13¼" squares, cutting each diagonally twice in an X for a total of 24 triangle pairs

3. Sew together a layered triangle pair along one of the short edges. (Be sure to sew the pairs with the same fabric on top and along the same short edge so all your pieced triangles will have the red-and-black check on the same side.) Press open, pressing the seam allowance toward the red-and-black check triangle, to make a pieced triangle. Repeat to make a total of 24 pieced triangles.

4. Join two pieced triangles to make an alternate block (see Diagram 4); press. The pieced alternate block should measure 12½" square, including the seam allowances. Repeat to make a total of 12 alternate blocks.

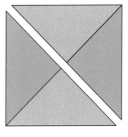

Diagram 4

Assemble the Quilt Top

Referring to the photograph *opposite top* for placement, lay out the 25 blocks in five horizontal rows, alternating Windblown Star and alternate blocks. Sew together the blocks in each row. Press the seam allowances toward the alternate blocks.

Then join the rows to complete the quilt center. The pieced quilt center should measure 60½" square, including the seam allowances.

Cut and Add the Borders

From red-and-black check, cut:
- 4—6½" squares for border corners

From black print, cut:
- 7—3½×42" strips for inner border

From red print No. 2, cut:
- 8—6½×42" strips for outer border

The following border strip measurements are mathematically correct. You may wish to make your border strips longer than specified to allow for possible sewing differences.

1. From the black print 3½×42" strips, piece:
   - 2—3½×60½" inner border strips
   - 2—3½×66½" inner border strips

2. Sew a short inner border strip to the top and bottom edges of the pieced quilt center. Then add a long inner border strip to each side edge of the pieced quilt center. Press the seam allowances toward the black print border.

3. From the red print 6½×42" strips, piece:
   - 4—6½×66½" outer border strips

4. Sew one outer border strip to the top and bottom edges of the pieced quilt center. Press the seam allowances toward the inner border.

5. Join a red-and-black check 6½" square border corner to each end of the two remaining red print outer border strips. Press the seam allowances toward the red print strips. Sew one pieced strip to each side edge of the pieced quilt center to complete the quilt top. Press the seam allowances toward the inner border.

Complete the Quilt

From black print, cut:
- 8—2×42" binding strips

1. Layer the quilt top, batting, and backing according to the instructions in Quilter's Schoolhouse, which begins on *page 145.*

2. Quilt as desired. This project was machine-quilted in an allover meandering pattern.

3. Use the black print 2×42" binding strips to bind the quilt according to the instructions in Quilter's Schoolhouse.

optional colors

The bold lines of the Lumberjack pattern suggested lively contemporary prints to quilt tester Laura Boehnke. She combined high-contrast colors with a black print and made a smaller quilt that contains five Windblown Star blocks and four alternate blocks.

continued

Lumberjack Quilt
optional sizes

If you'd like to make this quilt in a size other than given, use the information *below*.

Alternate quilt sizes	Wall	Queen	King
Number of Windblown Star blocks	5	21	32
Number of alternate blocks	4	21	32
Number of blocks wide by long	3×3	6×7	8×8
Finished size	54" square	90×102"	114" square
Yardage requirements			
Black check	1¼ yards	4 yards	5½ yards
Red print No. 1	⅝ yard	2½ yards	2¾ yards
Red-and-black check	¾ yard	1¾ yards	3 yards
Black print	⅞ yard	1½ yards	1⅞ yards
Red print No. 2	1 yard	1⅞ yards	2¼ yards
Backing	3⅓ yards	8 yards	10 yards
Batting	60" square	96×108"	120" square

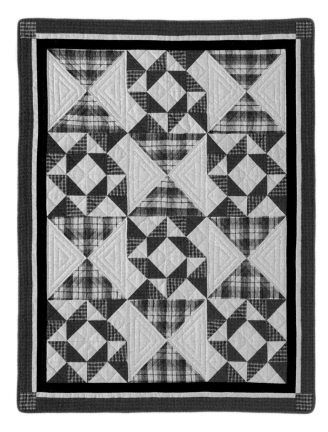

KID'S FLANNEL BRIGHTS QUILT

Any child would love to snuggle under this cozy throw. It's perfect to cuddle up with while reading a book or watching a favorite program.

Materials

1⅜ yards of red check flannel for blocks, border, and binding

1⅜ yards of yellow check flannel for blocks and border

½ yard of green check flannel for blocks and border corners

½ yard of multicolor plaid flannel for blocks

⅓ yard of solid dark blue flannel for inner border

2⅞ yards of flannel backing fabric

51×63" of quilt batting

Finished quilt top: 45×57"
Finished block: 12" square

Cut the Fabrics

To make the best use of your fabrics, cut the pieces in the order that follows. The border strip measurements are mathematically correct. You may wish to cut your border strips longer than specified to allow for possible sewing differences.

From red check flannel, cut:
- 3—3⅞×42" strips
- 5—2¾×42" strips for border
- 6—2½×42" binding strips

From yellow check flannel, cut:
- 1—13¼×42" strip
- 6—3⅞×42" strips
- 5—1¼×42" strips for border

From green check flannel, cut:
- 3—3⅞×42" strips
- 4—3" squares

From multicolor plaid flannel, cut:
- 1—13¼×42" strip

From solid dark blue flannel, cut:
- 5—2×42" strips for inner border

Assemble the Blocks

1. Referring to the Cut and Assemble the Windblown Star Blocks instructions on *page 50* and the photograph *above* for color placement, use three red check 3⅞×42" strips, six yellow check 3⅞×42"

strips, and three green check 3⅞×42" strips to make a total of six Windblown Star blocks.

2. Referring to the Cut and Assemble the Alternate Blocks instructions on *page 50*, use one yellow check 13¼×42" strip and one multicolor plaid 13¼×42" strip to make a total of six alternate blocks.

Assemble the Quilt Center

Referring to the photograph *opposite* for placement, lay out the blocks in four horizontal rows, alternating Windblown Star blocks and alternate blocks. Sew together the blocks in each row. Press the seam allowances toward the alternate blocks. Then join the rows to complete the quilt center. Press the seam allowances in one direction. The pieced quilt center should measure 36½×48½", including the seam allowances.

continued

Cut and Add the Borders

1. Cut and piece the solid dark blue flannel 2×42" strips to make the following:
   - 2—2×51½" inner border strips
   - 2—2×36½" inner border strips

2. Sew the short dark blue inner border strips to the top and bottom edges of the pieced quilt center. Then add a long dark blue inner border strip to the each side edge of the pieced quilt center. Press the seam allowances toward the dark blue border.

3. Cut and piece the yellow check flannel 1¼×42" strips to make the following:
   - 2—1¼×57½" border strips
   - 2—1¼×39½" border strips

4. Cut and piece the red check flannel 2¾×42" strips to make the following:
   - 2—2¾×57½" border strips
   - 2—2¾×39½" border strips

5. Sew together a yellow check 1¼×39½" border strip and a red check 2¾×39½" border strip to make a top border unit. Press the seam allowances to one side. Repeat to make a matching bottom border unit.

6. Sew a border unit to the top and bottom edges of the pieced quilt center. Press the seam allowances toward the border.

7. Sew together a yellow check 1¼×57½" border strip and a red check 2¾×57½" border strip to make a side border unit. Press the seam allowances to one side. Repeat to make a second side border unit.

8. Sew a green check 3" square to each end of the side border units. Press the seam allowances toward the border units. Sew a side border unit to each side edge of the pieced quilt center to complete the quilt top. Press the seam allowances toward the quilt center.

Complete the Quilt

1. Layer the quilt top, batting, and backing according to the instructions in Quilter's Schoolhouse, which begins on *page 145*. Quilt as desired.

2. Use the red check 2½×42½" strips to bind the quilt according to the instructions in Quilter's Schoolhouse.

PICNIC CLOTH

Celebrate summertime with a picnic blanket that shows off your patriotic spirit. After you've pieced it, stitch a field of stars onto the blue blocks and curving stripes running across the red blocks for a flag-waving finish.

Materials

½ yard of dark blue star print for blocks

1¾ yards of cream-and-red star print for blocks

1¼ yards total of assorted red prints for blocks

⅜ yard of gold print for inner border

½ yard of red print for middle border

1 yard of dark blue print for outer border and binding

3⅝ yards of backing fabric

64" square of quilt batting or flannel

Finished quilt top: 58" square
Finished block: 12" square

Cut the Fabrics

To make the best use of your fabrics, cut the pieces in the order that follows. The border strip measurements are mathematically correct. You may wish to cut your border strips longer than specified to allow for possible sewing differences.

Simple Sensations

From dark blue star print, cut:
- 1—13¼×42" strip

From cream-and-red star print, cut:
- 4—13¼×42" strips

From assorted red prints, cut:
- 3—13¼×42" strips

From gold print, cut:
- 5—1½×42" strips for inner border

From red print, cut:
- 6—2¼×42" strips for middle border

From dark blue print, cut:
- 6—2¾×42" strips for outer border
- 6—2½×42" binding strips

Assemble the Blocks

Referring to the Cut and Assemble the Alternate Blocks instructions on *page 50*, use the dark blue star print 13¼×42" strip, the four cream-and-red star print 13¼×42" strips, and the three assorted red print 13¼×42" strips to make a total of 16 alternate blocks. Make four dark blue and cream-and-red star print blocks and 12 red print and cream-and-red star print blocks.

Assemble the Quilt Center

Referring to the photograph at *right* for placement, lay out blocks in four horizontal rows of four blocks each. Sew together the blocks in each row. Press the seam allowances in one direction, alternating the direction with each row. Then join the rows to complete the quilt center. Press the seam allowances in one direction. The pieced quilt center should measure 48½" square, including the seam allowances.

Piece and Add the Borders

1. Cut and piece the gold print 1½×42" strips to make the following:
   - 2—1½×50½" inner border strips
   - 2—1½×48½" inner border strips

2. Sew a short inner border strip to the top and bottom edges of the pieced quilt center. Join a long inner border strip to each side edge of the pieced quilt center. Press the seam allowances toward the inner border.

3. Cut and piece the red print 2¼×42" strips to make the following:
   - 2—2¼×50½" middle border strips
   - 2—2¼×54" middle border strips

4. Sew a short middle border strip to the top and bottom edges of the pieced quilt center. Join a long middle border strip to each side edge of the pieced quilt center. Press the seam allowances toward the middle border.

5. Cut and piece the dark blue print 2¾×42" strips to make the following:
   - 2—2¾×58½" outer border strips
   - 2—2¾×54" outer border strips

6. Sew a short outer border strip to the top and bottom edges of the pieced quilt center. Join a long outer border strip to each side edge of the pieced quilt center to complete the quilt top. Press the seam allowances toward the outer border.

Complete the Quilt

1. Layer the quilt top, batting or flannel, and backing according to the instructions in Quilter's Schoolhouse, which begins on *page 145*.

2. Quilt as desired. This project was hand-quilted with utility stitches. Stars were stitched on the dark blue star print blocks. Curving stripes that mimic flag stripes were stitched on the rest of the quilt.

3. Use the dark blue print 2½×42½" strips to bind the quilt according to the instructions in Quilter's Schoolhouse.

COLORFUL CREATIONS

Do your quilts need a bit more flavor? Spice them up with a dash of vibrant colors. The recipe for the quilts in this chapter is simple. Take a favorite pattern, mix in an assortment of brightly-hued fabrics, garnish with a dynamic quilting technique, and voilà—you'll have a beautiful project that will leave you hungry for more.

Becky Goldsmith and Linda Jenkins

of Piece O' Cake Designs designed this quilt

for the Sixth Annual Sampler Quilt Series™ that appeared

in American Patchwork & Quilting® magazine in 1998.

THERE GOES THE
Neighborhood

Materials

1¾ yards total of assorted black-and-white prints for appliqué foundations and sashing

1 yard total of assorted bright prints in red, blue, purple, green, yellow, and white for house and bird appliqués and sashing

Scraps of assorted brown prints for house appliqués

¼ yard of multicolor stripe for inner border

1 yard of multicolor star print for outer border

¼ yard of multicolor ribbon print for outer border corners

½ yard of orange-and-yellow mottled print for letter and number appliqués

¾ yard of orange print for cording cover

3⅛ yards of backing fabric

56" square of quilt batting

6 yards of ¼"-wide cotton cording

Green embroidery floss

9—⅜"-diameter buttons in assorted colors for doorknobs

Assorted specialty buttons, glass beads, and a miniature strand of holiday lights for block embellishments

1½ yards of clear upholstery vinyl *or* other clear, flexible plastic (optional)

continued

Finished quilt top: 50" square
Finished block: 10" square

Quantities specified for 44/45"-wide, 100% cotton fabrics. All measurements include a ¼" seam allowance. Sew with right sides together unless otherwise stated.

Select an Appliqué Method

Over the years, project designers Becky Goldsmith and Linda Jenkins have developed their own appliqué method, which uses an overlay of clear upholstery vinyl for placement purposes. The following instructions are for their overlay method. Your favorite appliqué technique also can be used.

Make Templates for Appliqué

1. The patterns are on *Pattern Sheets 1* and *2*. Make templates of pattern pieces 1 through 30, following the instructions in Quilter's Schoolhouse, which begins on *page 145*. Mark the right side of each template with its corresponding number. The numbers indicate the appliquéing sequence.

2. Cut out the templates on the drawn lines with sharp scissors. Becky and Linda stress the importance of keeping template edges smooth and points sharp so that the resultant appliqué edges and points will be precise.

Cut the Fabrics

To make the best use of your fabrics, cut the pieces in the order that follows. The inner border strip measurements are mathematically correct. You may wish to cut your inner border strips longer than specified to allow for possible sewing differences.

When cutting out the appliqué pieces, lay the fabrics and templates with right sides up; trace. Add ¼" seam allowances to pieces 1 through 4 because they will be machine-pieced. Add a ³⁄₁₆" seam allowance to the remaining pieces because they will be appliquéd.

The appliqué foundations are cut larger than necessary to allow for possible sewing differences. You'll trim the foundations to the correct size after completing the appliqué.

From assorted black-and-white prints, cut:
- 9—11½" squares for appliqué foundations
- 36—1½×10½" sashing strips

From assorted bright red, blue, purple, and green prints, cut:
- 36—1½" squares for sashing
- 9 *each* of patterns 1, 2, 3, and 4

From assorted bright blue prints, cut:
- 1 *each* of patterns 28, 28 reversed, 29, and 29 reversed

From assorted bright yellow prints, cut:
- 9 *each* of patterns 5 and 6
- 2 of Pattern 27

From assorted white prints, cut:
- 2 of Pattern 30

From assorted brown print scraps, cut:
- 9 of Pattern 7

From multicolor stripe, cut:
- 4—1½×40" inner border strips

From multicolor star print, cut:
- 4—8×40" outer border strips

From multicolor ribbon print, cut:
- 4—6½" squares

From orange-and-yellow mottled print, cut:
- 4—8×14" strips

From orange print, cut:
- 1—27" square, cutting it into enough 1½"-wide bias strips to total 210" in length for cording (For specific instructions, see Cut Bias Strips in Quilter's Schoolhouse, which begins on *page 145*.)

Piece and Appliqué the Blocks

1. Cut a 10" square from the clear upholstery vinyl or other clear, flexible plastic. Position the clear square over the House Block Appliqué Placement Diagram on *Pattern Sheet 2*, and accurately trace the design with a permanent marker.

2. Referring to the diagram at *right*, lay out one each of pieces 1 through 4. Sew together the pieces in sections. Press the seam allowances toward pieces 1 and 3. Then join the sections to make a pieced house unit. Press the seam allowance in one direction.

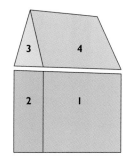

House Assembly Diagram

3. Center the overlay on a black-and-white print appliqué foundation 11½" square. Pin the top of the overlay to the fabric, if desired.

4. Slide the pieced house unit, right side up, between the foundation square and the overlay. When the pieced house unit is in place, remove the overlay, pin the pieced house unit to the foundation, and appliqué it in place.

5. Use the overlay to position one each of bright yellow print pieces 5 and 6 and brown print piece 7 on the pieced house unit. Pin the pieces in place; appliqué them to the house unit.

6. Repeat steps 1 through 5 to make a total of nine house blocks.

Embellish the House Blocks

Becky and Linda embellished each house block with fabric appliqués, embroidery stitches, assorted buttons, beads, and/or miniature lights. Their embellishments for each block—numbering them from left to right and top to bottom—follow (see the detail photographs). Specific button shapes are identified under each house block for your reference. Substitute your choice of novelty buttons as desired. Work in numerical order when adding appliqué pieces to blocks. Add all hard embellishments after quilting the top to prevent them from getting caught in stitching lines or being damaged.

House Block No. 1

From brown print, cut:
- 1 of Pattern 8

From assorted bright green prints, cut:
- 1 *each* of patterns 9, 10, and 11

1. Position the appliqué pieces on the house block. Pin and appliqué them in place to create a trimmed bush.

2. Stitch a miniature strand of holiday lights below the roofline.

House Block No. 2
From assorted bright prints, cut:
- 1 *each* of patterns 12 and 13

1. Position the appliqué pieces on the house block. Pin and appliqué them in place to create flower boxes.

2. Using two strands of green embroidery floss, backstitch flower stems and leaves above the flower boxes. Stitch buttons and beads to the top of each embroidered flower stem.

House Block No. 3
From bright green print, cut:
- 1 of Pattern 14

From bright red print, cut:
- 1 of Pattern 15

1. Position the appliqué pieces on the house block. Pin and appliqué them in place to create a wreath.

2. Stitch assorted glass beads below the roofline.

House Block No. 4

Stitch a glass wreath-shape button above the door on the house block. Stitch a clay cat-shape button beside the door.

House Block No. 5
From assorted bright red prints, cut:
- 1 *each* of patterns 16, 17, 18, and 19

1. Position the appliqué pieces on the house block. Be sure the bottom edge of piece 16 extends into the seam allowance. Pin and appliqué them in place to create a mailbox. Using two strands of red embroidery floss, backstitch a flagpole.

2. Stitch two clay package-shape buttons below the mailbox.

continued

House Block No. 6

From brown print, cut:
- 1 of Pattern 20

From bright green print, cut:
- 1 of Pattern 21

1. Position the appliqué pieces on the house block. Pin and appliqué them in place to create a tree.

2. Stitch a ceramic flowerpot-shape button on each side of the door. Stitch red beads to the tree.

House Block No. 7

From brown print, cut:
- 1 of Pattern 22

From bright green print, cut:
- 1 of Pattern 23

From bright purple print, cut:
- 1 of Pattern 24

1. Position the appliqué pieces on the house block. Pin and appliqué them in place to create a tree and chimney.

2. Stitch metallic star-shape beads to the tree.

House Block No. 8

From assorted bright yellow prints, cut:
- 1 *each* of patterns 25 and 26

1. Position the appliqué pieces on the house block. Pin and appliqué them in place to create a sun.

2. Stitch assorted glass beads around each window. Stitch a ceramic bird-shape button above the door.

House Block No. 9

Using two strands of green embroidery floss, backstitch flower stems and leaves along the bottom of the house. Stitch buttons to the top of each embroidered flower stem.

Finish the Blocks

Press and trim each appliquéd house block to measure 10½" square, including the seam allowances.

Add the Block Sashing

1. Sew the black-and-white print 1½×10½" sashing strips to the top and bottom edges of each house block. Press the seam allowances toward the sashing strips.

2. Sew a bright print 1½" sashing square to each end of the remaining black-and-white print 1½×10½" sashing strips to make 1½×12½" pieced sashing strips. Press the seam allowances toward the black-and-white sashing strips. Sew the pieced sashing strips to the side edges of each house block. Press the seam allowances toward the sashing strips. Each sashed house block should measure 12½" square, including the seam allowances.

Assemble the Quilt Center

Referring to the photograph on *page 58* for placement, lay out the nine house blocks in three horizontal rows. Sew together the blocks in each row. Press the seam allowances in each row in one direction, alternating the direction with each row. Join the rows to make the quilt center. Press the seam allowances in one direction. The pieced quilt center should measure 36½" square, including the seam allowances.

Add the Inner Border

1. With the midpoints aligned, pin a multicolor stripe 1½×40" inner border strip to each edge of the pieced quilt center; allow the excess border fabric to extend beyond the edges. Sew together, beginning and ending the seams ¼" from the corners. Press the seam allowances toward the border strips.

2. Complete the inner border by mitering the corners. For information on mitering, see the instructions in Quilter's Schoolhouse, which begins on *page 145*.

Appliqué the Outer Border

Becky and Linda used reverse appliqué to add the letters and numbers to the outer border. In reverse appliqué, you cut away the top fabric to reveal the fabric underneath.

The birds were appliquéd using their overlay appliqué technique.

The outer border strips are larger than necessary to allow for possible sewing differences. You'll trim the outer border strips to the correct size after completing the appliqué and reverse appliqué.

1. Make a template for each letter and number needed (see *Pattern Sheet 2*). Then make an overlay for each word (Love, Faith, and Hope) and an overlay for the year with a bird on either side of the numbers. Space the letters and numbers carefully, use a straight baseline to keep them straight, and mark the center points.

2. With midpoints aligned, position the "Love" overlay over a multicolor star print 8×40" outer border strip. Pin the overlay in place. Slide the templates, one at a time, under the overlay into position. Using white chalk, carefully trace around each template on the outer border strip (see Photo 1, *right*).

3. Place an orange-and-yellow mottled print 8×14" strip right side up directly under where the letters were traced on the outer border strip. Baste around the outer edge of each letter, 5/16" away from the traced lines (see Photo 2, *right*).

4. Starting in the middle of the first letter, cut away a small portion of the outer border fabric, leaving 3/16" to turn under. Turn the raw edge under and slip-stitch the folded edge to the mottled fabric below (see Photo 3, *right*). Cut away more, a little at a time, until you have revealed the entire letter and stitched its folded edge down (see Photo 4, *right*). Once you've completed the appliqué, trim away the orange-and-yellow mottled print strip underneath so that just a 1/4" seam allowance remains around each letter.

5. Repeat steps 2 through 4 for "Faith," "Hope," and the year on the remaining multicolor star print 8×40" outer border strips.

6. Reposition the year border overlay on the border strip. Pin the top of the overlay to the fabric, if desired.

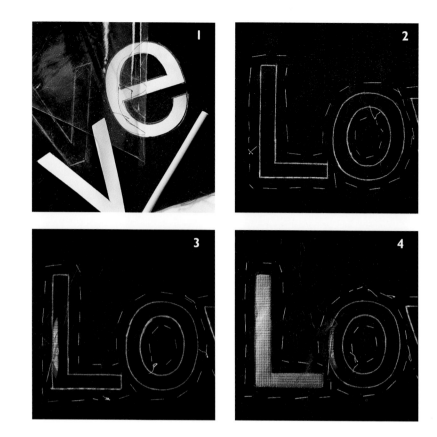

7. Slide the appliqué pieces for the birds between the border strip and the overlay. When the bird pieces are in place, remove the overlay, pin the bird pieces to the border, and appliqué them in place.

8. When appliquéing is complete, press the outer border strips from behind and trim each strip to measure 6½×38½", including the seam allowances. Be careful when trimming the strips to size to make sure the words remain centered.

Add the Outer Border

1. Sew the "Faith" border strip to the top edge of the quilt center and the year border strip to the bottom edge. Press the seam allowances toward the outer border strips.

2. Sew a multicolor ribbon print 6½" square to each end of the remaining outer border strips.

3. Sew the "Love" border strip to the left edge of the quilt center and the "Hope" border strip to the right edge to complete the quilt top. Press the seam allowances toward the outer border strips.

continued

Complete the Quilt

1. Join the orange print 1½"-wide bias strips to make a 210"-long strip.

2. With the wrong side inside, fold under 1½" at one end of the strip. With the wrong side inside, fold the strip in half lengthwise to make the cording cover. Insert the cording next to the folded edge, placing a cording end 1" from the cording cover folded end. Using a machine cording foot, sew through both fabric layers right next to the cording.

3. Starting on one side of the quilt top, align raw edges and stitch the covered cording to the right side of the quilt top. Begin stitching 1½" from the cording's folded end. Round the corners slightly, making sure the corner curves match. As you stitch each corner, gently ease the covered cording into place.

4. When the covered cording has been stitched around the entire edge of the quilt top, cut the cording so that it will fit snugly into the folded opening at the beginning. The ends of the cording should abut inside the orange print cover. Stitch the ends down and trim raw edges as needed.

5. Layer the quilt top, batting, and backing according to the instructions in Quilter's Schoolhouse, which begins on *page 145*.

6. Quilt as desired, leaving about 2–3" of the outer edge unquilted to allow for turning the cording later. Becky machine-quilted each house block differently. If a stripe fabric was used, she followed the lines in the fabric. She also used a meandering pattern in several places. She quilted a scalloped pattern in each roof.

7. Trim the batting even with the cording seam line. Trim the backing even with the outer raw edge of the quilt top, ¼" larger than the batting on all sides. Fold the cording cover seam allowance over the batting. Fold under the quilt backing; whipstitch the edges together. Quilt the remaining portion of the quilt top.

8. Sew an assorted-color ⅜"-diameter button to the brown print piece of each house block as a doorknob. Add any remaining hard embellishments as previously detailed.

There Goes the Neighborhood Quilt
optional sizes

If you'd like to make the quilt in a size other than given, use the information *below*.

Alternate quilt sizes	Small Wall	Lap	Large Wall
Number of blocks	4	12	16
Number of blocks wide by long	2×2	3×4	4×4
Finished size	38" square	50×62"	62" square
Yardage requirements			
Assorted black-and-white prints	⅞ yard	2 yards	3 yards
Total of assorted bright prints	¾ yard	1 yard	1½ yards
Assorted brown prints	Scraps	Scraps	Scraps
Multicolor stripe	¼ yard	⅓ yard	⅜ yard
Multicolor star print	1 yard	1¼ yards	1½ yards
Multicolor ribbon print	¼ yard	¼ yard	¼ yard
Orange-and-yellow mottled print	½ yard	½ yard	½ yard
Orange print	¾ yard	¾ yard	¾ yard
Backing	1¼ yards	3⅛ yards	3¾ yards
Batting	42" square	56×68"	68" square
¼"-wide cotton cording	5 yards	7 yards	8 yards

HOUSE PILLOW

Whether you make it for yourself, as a housewarming gift, or to give to a friend, this charming country pillow will find a comfy spot in any home.

Materials

¹⁄₃ yard of cream print for appliqué foundation

Scraps of assorted rust prints for appliqués and sashing

Scraps of assorted navy prints for appliqués and sashing

Scraps of assorted gold prints for appliqués

Scrap of dark brown print for appliqué

Scrap of dark green print for appliqué and sashing

Scraps of assorted tan prints for sashing

¹⁄₈ yard of brown-and-black print for sashing

¹⁄₄ yard of navy-and-black print for flange

18¹⁄₂" square of fabric for pillow back

24" square of quilt backing

24" square of quilt batting

14" pillow form

Black perle cotton thread

Finished pillow: 14" square, plus a 2" flange on all sides
Finished block: 10" square

Cut the Fabrics

To make the best use of your fabrics, cut the pieces in the order that follows. The sashing, border, and flange strip measurements are mathematically correct. You may wish to cut your strips longer than specified to allow for possible sewing differences.

This project uses "There Goes the Neighborhood" patterns, which are on *Pattern Sheet 1.* To make templates of the patterns, follow the instructions in Quilter's Schoolhouse, which begins on *page 145.* When cutting out the appliqué pieces, lay the fabric and templates right sides up; trace. Add ¹⁄₄" seam allowances to pieces 1 though 4, because they will be machine-pieced. Add a ³⁄₁₆" seam allowance to the remaining pieces because they will be appliquéd.

From cream print, cut:
- 1—11¹⁄₂" square for appliqué foundation

From assorted rust prints, cut:
- 1 *each* of patterns 1 and 2
- 8—1¹⁄₂" squares for sashing

From assorted navy prints, cut:
- 1 *each* of patterns 3 and 4
- 4—1¹⁄₂" squares for sashing

From assorted gold prints, cut:
- 1 *each* of patterns 5, 6, and 7

From dark brown print, cut:
- 1 of Pattern 20

From dark green print, cut:
- 1 of Pattern 21
- 4—1¹⁄₂" squares for sashing

continued

From assorted tan scraps, cut:
- 4—1½×10½" sashing strips

From brown-and-black print, cut:
- 4—1½×10½" sashing strips

From navy-and-black print, cut:
- 2—2½×18½" flange strips
- 2—2½×14½" flange strips

Piece and Appliqué the Block

1. Referring to the Piece and Appliqué the Blocks instructions on *page 60* and the photograph on *page 65*, use pieces 1 through 7 and the tan print 11½" appliqué foundation to assemble one house block.

2. Pin pieces 20 and 21 to the house block. Using black perle cotton, blanket-stitch the appliqué pieces in place.

   To blanket-stitch, first pull the needle up at A (see diagram *below*). Form a reverse L shape with the floss, and hold the angle of the L shape in place with your thumb. Push the needle down at B and come up at C to secure the stitch. Repeat until you've stitched around the shape.

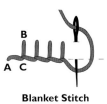

Blanket Stitch

3. Press and trim the appliquéd house block to measure 10½" square, including the seam allowances.

Add the Block Sashing

1. Sew the tan print 1½×10½" sashing strips to the top and bottom edges of the house block. Press the seam allowances toward the sashing strips.

2. Sew a rust print 1½" sashing square to each end of the remaining tan print 1½×10½" sashing strips to make 1½×12½" pieced sashing strips. Press the seam allowances toward the tan print sashing strips. Sew the pieced sashing strips to the side edges of the house block. Press the seam allowances toward the sashing strips. The sashed house block should measure 12½" square, including the seam allowances.

3. Sew a navy print 1½" sashing square to each end of a brown-and-black print 1½×10½" sashing strip. Repeat to make a matching pieced strip. Sew these pieced strips to the top and bottom edges of the sashed house block. Press the seam allowances toward the brown-and-black sashing.

4. Join a dark green print 1½" sashing square and a rust print 1½" sashing square. Repeat to make a total of four dark-green-and-rust print pairs. Then sew the dark green end of a pair to each end of the remaining brown-and-black print 1½×10½" sashing strips. Sew these pieced strips to each side edge of the sashed house block. Press the seam allowances toward the brown-and-black sashing.

Finish the Pillow

1. Sew a navy-and-black print 2½×14½" flange strip to each side edge of the sashed house block. Then add a navy-and-black print 2½×18½" flange strip to the top and bottom edges of the sashed house block to complete the pillow top. Press all seam allowances toward the navy-and-black print flange.

2. Layer the pillow top, batting, and quilt backing according to the instructions in Quilter's Schoolhouse, which begins on *page 145*. Quilt as desired. Using black perle cotton and a running stitch, embroider "Est. 2002" (or the year of your choice) to the inner sashing on the right side of the house block. Trim the batting and backing to measure 18½" square, including the seam allowances.

3. With right sides together, sew together the quilted pillow top and the 18½" square pillow back, leaving an opening for the pillow form along a side edge to make the pillow cover. Turn the pillow cover right side out. Stitch in the ditch between the sashing and the flange around three sides, leaving open the same side edge as was left open for the pillow form.

4. Insert the pillow form through the opening. Stitch in the ditch on the unstitched side between the sashing and flange. Whipstitch the outer seam opening closed.

Colorful Creations

ANNIVERSARY QUILT

*Capture a lifetime of memories on fabric
with a photo transfer quilt. Make one to
celebrate an anniversary or graduation or
to commemorate a baby's first year.*

Materials

⅓ yard of taupe print for appliqué foundation

¼ yard of white print for appliqués and sashing

½ yard of solid cream for blocks

½ yard total of assorted taupe and tan prints for
   blocks and photo section border

¼ yard of brown print for inner border

½ yard of dark taupe print No. 1 for outer border

⅜ yard of dark taupe print No. 2 for binding

1½ yards of backing fabric

37×54" of batting

Photo transfer paper

Color photocopies of 14 pictures

continued

Finished quilt: 30½×48½"

About Photo Transfers

Photo transfer paper, available in quilt shops and photocopying shops, does what its name implies; it transfers photographic images onto fabric. The process involves two steps—photocopying a picture onto transfer paper, then ironing the transfer-paper image onto fabric. For this quilt, the sepia-tone look was achieved by copying the photos using brown toner.

Transfer papers require a sophisticated color photocopier that can produce a good quality mirror image. Not every copy shop is willing to make photo transfers or to use transfer paper you've purchased elsewhere; some copy shops offer their own photo-transfer services. It's also possible to get your photos transferred via mail-order suppliers.

Cut the Fabrics

To make the best use of your fabrics, cut the pieces in the order that follows. The border strip measurements are mathematically correct. You may wish to cut your border strips longer than specified to allow for possible sewing differences.

This project uses "There Goes the Neighborhood" patterns, which are on *Pattern Sheet 2*. To make templates of the patterns, follow the instructions in

Quilter's Schoolhouse, which begins on *page 145*. Add a ³⁄₁₆" seam allowance when cutting out the pattern pieces because they will be appliquéd.

The appliqué foundation is cut larger than necessary to allow for possible sewing differences. You'll trim the foundation to the correct size after completing the appliqué.

From taupe print, cut:
- 1—9×44" appliqué foundation (will trim to finished size later)

From white print, cut:
- 1 *each* of patterns A, F, I, L, P, T, uppercase H, lowercase H, and V
- 2 *each* of patterns E and O
- 1—1½×42½" sashing strip

From solid cream, cut:
- 14—4½×6½" rectangles

From assorted taupe and tan prints, cut:
- 2—2¼×15½" photo section border strips
- 28—1¼×8" rectangles
- 28—1¼×4½" rectangles

From brown print, cut:
- 2—1¼×42½" inner border strips
- 2—1¼×26" inner border strips

From dark taupe print No. 1, cut:
- 3—3×42" outer border strips
- 2—3×31" outer border strips

From dark taupe print No. 2, cut:
- 4—2½×42" binding strips

Appliqué the Panel

1. To create the appliquéd side panel, you need the taupe print 9×44" appliqué foundation, one *each* of white print appliqué pieces A, F, I, L, P, T, and V, and two *each* of white print E, H, and O.

2. Prepare all the appliqué pieces by basting under the ³⁄₁₆" seam allowances.

3. Referring to the photograph *opposite* for placement, arrange and baste the appliqué letters for the words "Love," "Faith," and "Hope" on the taupe print appliqué foundation. Space letters and words carefully and keep them on a straight baseline 2½" above the bottom edge of the appliqué foundation.

4. Using small slip stitches and thread that matches the fabric, appliqué the pieces to the foundation.

5. Trim the appliquéd panel to 8½x42", including the seam allowances.

Assemble the Blocks

1. Transfer a photograph onto each solid cream 4½x6½" rectangle according to the photo transfer paper manufacturer's instructions.

2. Sew an assorted taupe or tan print 1¼x4½" rectangle to each side edge of a cream photo-transferred rectangle. Join an assorted taupe or tan print 1¼x8" rectangle to the top and bottom edges of the cream photo-transferred rectangle to make a photo block. Press all seam allowances toward the outside. The photo block should now measure 6x8" including the seam allowances.

3. Repeat Step 2 to make a total of 14 photo blocks.

Assemble the Block Rows

Referring to the photograph at *right* for placement, lay out the photo blocks in seven horizontal rows; sew together. Press the seam allowances in one direction, alternating the direction with each row; join the rows to make the photo section. Add one taupe or tan print 2¼x15½" photo section border strip to the top and bottom edges. The pieced photo section should measure 15½x42½", including the seam allowances.

Assemble the Quilt Center

Referring to the photograph at *right*, lay out the appliquéd panel, the white print 1½x42½" sashing strip, and the pieced photo section; sew together to make the quilt center. Press the seam allowances in one direction. The pieced quilt center should measure 24½x42½", including the seam allowances.

Add the Borders

1. Sew a brown print 1¼x42½" inner border strip to each side edge of the pieced quilt center. Then add a brown print 1¼x26" inner border strip to the top and bottom edges of the pieced quilt center. Press all seam allowances toward the inner border. The pieced quilt center should now measure 26x44", including the seam allowances.

2. From dark taupe print No. 1 3x12" strips, cut and piece the following:
  • 2—3x44" outer border strips

3. Sew one dark taupe 3x44" outer border strip to each side edge of the quilt. Then add one dark taupe 3x31" outer border strip to the top and bottom edges of the pieced quilt center to complete the quilt top. Press all seam allowances toward the outer border.

Complete the Quilt Top

1. Layer the quilt top, batting, and backing according to the instructions in Quilter's Schoolhouse, which begins on *page 145*. Quilt as desired.

2. Use the dark taupe print 2½x42" strips to bind the quilt according to the instructions in Quilter's Schoolhouse.

COLORFUL
Cakes

Fabric designer Jennifer Sampou and quilt shop owner Carolie Hensley,

who also happens to be Jennifer's mother-in-law, joined creative forces to design

this cheerful wall hanging. Using more than 70 fabrics, they transformed

the traditional Cake Stand block into a contemporary work of art.

Colorful Creations

Materials

70—18×22" pieces (fat quarters) of assorted light, medium, and dark prints for blocks and binding

¾ yard of gold print for setting and corner triangles

2⅞ yards of backing fabric

51×63" of quilt batting

Finished quilt top: 45×56¼"
Finished block: 8" square

Quantities specified for 44/45"-wide, 100% cotton fabrics. All measurements include a ¼" seam allowance. Sew with right sides together unless otherwise stated.

Designer Notes

Jennifer Sampou and Carolie Hensley chose prints with multiple layers of color, which gave the quilt depth and movement.

Traditionally, this block is made with two fabrics—one for all the cake-stand pieces and one for the background. Although Jennifer used only two fabrics in several blocks, she mixed and matched both the cake-stand pieces and the background pieces to add interest to the finished project.

Cut the Fabrics

To make the best use of your fabrics, cut the pieces in the order that follows.

The setting triangles and corner triangles are cut slightly larger than necessary. You'll trim them to the correct size after piecing the quilt top.

continued

From assorted light and medium prints, cut:
- 16—4⅞" squares, cutting each in half diagonally for a total of 32 large triangles
- 96—2⅞" squares, cutting each in half diagonally for a total of 192 small triangles
- 192—2½" squares
- 7—2½×18" binding strips

From assorted medium and dark prints, cut:
- 16—4⅞" squares, cutting each in half diagonally for a total of 32 large triangles
- 96—2⅞" squares, cutting each in half diagonally for a total of 192 small triangles
- 7—2½×18" binding strips

From gold print, cut:
- 4—12¾" squares, cutting each diagonally twice in an X for a total of 16 setting triangles (there will be 2 left over)
- 2—6¾" squares, cutting each in half diagonally for a total of 4 corner triangles

Assemble the Cake Stand Blocks

1. For one Cake Stand block you'll need six light or medium print small triangles, six medium or dark print small triangles, one light or medium print large triangle, one medium or dark print large triangle, and six light or medium print 2½" squares.

2. Join one light or medium print small triangle and one medium or dark print small triangle to make a small triangle-square (see Diagram 1). Press the seam allowance toward the darker triangle. The pieced small triangle-square should measure 2½" square, including the seam allowances. Repeat to make a total of six small triangle-squares.

Diagram 1

3. Sew together one light or medium print large triangle and one medium or dark print large triangle to make a large triangle-square. Press the seam allowance toward the darker triangle. The pieced large triangle-square should measure 4½" square, including the seam allowances.

4. Referring to Diagram 2 for placement, sew together two pairs of small triangle-squares. Press the seam allowances in one direction. Sew one small triangle-square pair to the top edge of the large triangle-square. Press the seam allowance toward the large triangle-square. Join a light or medium print 2½" square to a dark edge of the remaining small triangle-square pair to make a vertical row. Press the seam allowances toward the light or medium print square. Then add the vertical row to the right edge of the large triangle-square. Press the seam allowance toward the large triangle-square.

Diagram 2

5. Referring to Diagram 3, sew together one small triangle-square and two light or medium print 2½" squares to make a horizontal row. Press the seam allowances in one direction. Sew the row to the bottom edge of the large triangle-square. Press the seam allowance toward the large triangle-square.

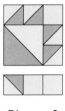

Diagram 3

6. Referring to Diagram 4, lay out the remaining three light or medium print 2½" squares and the remaining small triangle-square in a vertical row; join. Press the seam allowances in one direction. Then sew the vertical row to the left edge of the large triangle-square to complete a Cake Stand block. Press the seam allowance toward the large triangle-square. The pieced Cake Stand block should measure 8½" square, including the seam allowances.

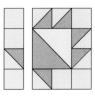

Diagram 4

Colorful Creations

7. Repeat steps 1 through 6 to make a total of 32 Cake Stand blocks.

Assemble the Quilt Top
1. Referring to the Quilt Assembly Diagram, lay out the 32 pieced Cake Stand blocks and 14 gold print setting triangles in diagonal rows.

2. Sew together the pieces in each diagonal row. Press the seam allowances in one direction, alternating the direction with each row. Then join the rows. Press the seam allowances in one direction.

3. Add the gold print corner triangles to complete the quilt top. Press the seam allowances toward the gold print corner triangles. Trim the setting and corner triangles, leaving a ¼" seam allowance beyond the block corners.

Complete the Quilt
1. Layer the quilt top, batting, and backing according to the instructions in Quilter's Schoolhouse, which begins on *page 145.*

2. Quilt as desired. This quilt was machine-quilted in an allover meandering pattern.

3. Use the assorted light, medium, and dark print 2½×18" strips to bind the quilt according to the instructions in Quilter's Schoolhouse.

Quilt Assembly Diagram

optional colors

The Cake Stand block first became popular in the 1920s and '30s. With today's reproduction fabrics, quilt tester Laura Boehnke was able to re-create this vintage look. Check your local quilt shop for various reproduction collections.

continued

Colorful Cakes Quilt
optional sizes

If you'd like to make the quilt in a size other than given, use the information *below*.

Alternate quilt sizes	Crib/Lap	Full/Queen	King
Number of blocks	18	98	145
Number of blocks wide by long	3×4	7×8	9×9
Finished size	34⅛×45½"	79⅝×91"	102⅜" square
Yardage requirements			
Assorted light, medium, and dark prints	2½ yards total	9⅛ yards total	13½ yards total
Gold print	¾ yard	1¼ yards	1¼ yards
Backing	1½ yards	7¼ yards	9⅛ yards
Batting	41×52"	86×97"	109" square

TEA TRAY

Your guests will delight at the beautiful quilted piece beneath the glass on this elegant tea tray. Along with the companion Tea Cozy on page 77, it will showcase your passion for quilting.

Materials

¼ yard of pink-and-blue floral for blocks

¼ yard of white print for blocks and inner border

⅜ yard of pink toile for block setting

⅛ yard of light pink for middle border

⅛ yard of pink print for outer border

Dark green mat and white mat

18¾×30½" burl wood frame

Two screw-mounted brass drawer pulls

Finished quilt top: 14⅜×25¾"
Finished block: 8" square

Cut the Fabrics

To make the best use of your fabrics, cut the pieces in the order that follows.

The setting and corner triangles are cut slightly larger than necessary. They will be trimmed to the correct size after piecing the quilt center.

From pink-and-blue floral, cut:
- 1—4⅞" square, cutting it in half diagonally for a total of 2 large triangles
- 6—2⅞" squares, cutting each in half diagonally for a total of 12 small triangles

From white print, cut:
- 1—4⅞" square, cutting it in half diagonally for a total of 2 large triangles
- 6—2⅞" squares, cutting each in half diagonally for a total of 12 small triangles
- 12—2½" squares
- 2—1×24¼" inner border strips
- 2—1×11⅞" inner border strips

From pink toile, cut:
- 2—6¾" squares, cutting each in half diagonally for a total of 4 corner triangles
- 1—12¾" square, cutting it diagonally twice in an X for a total of 4 setting triangles (there will be 2 left over)

From light pink print, cut:

- 2—1×25¼" middle border strips
- 2—1×12⅞" middle border strips

From pink print, cut:

- 2—1×26¼" outer border strips
- 2—1×13⅞" outer border strips

Assemble the Cake Stand Blocks

Referring to the Assemble the Cake Stand Blocks instructions on *page 72*, use six pink-and-blue floral small triangles, six white print small triangles, one pink-and-blue floral large triangle, one white print large triangle, and six white print 2½" squares to make a Cake Stand block. Repeat to make a total of two Cake Stand blocks.

Assemble the Quilt Top

1. Referring to the Quilt Assembly Diagram for placement, pair each pieced Cake Stand block with a pink toile setting triangle; sew together in pairs. Press the seam allowances in one direction, alternating the direction with each row.

2. Join the pairs. Press the seam allowances in one direction. Add the four pink toile corner triangles

Quilt Assembly Diagram

to complete the quilt center. Press the seam allowances toward the pink toile triangles.

3. Trim the setting and corner triangles to square up the quilt center, leaving a ¼" seam allowance beyond the block corners. The pieced quilt center should measure 11⅞×23¼", including the seam allowances.

Add the Borders

1. Sew a white print 1×11⅞" inner border strip to each side edge of the pieced quilt center. Then add a white print 1×24¼" inner border strip to the top and bottom edges of the pieced quilt center. Press the seam allowances toward the inner border.

continued

2. Join a light pink print 1×12⅞" middle border strip to each side edge of the pieced quilt center. Then add a light pink print 1×25¼" middle border strip to the top and bottom edges of the pieced quilt center. Press the seam allowances toward the middle border.

3. Sew a pink print 1×13⅞" outer border strip to each side edge of the pieced quilt center. Then join a pink print 1×26¼" outer border strip to the top and bottom edges of the pieced quilt center to complete the quilt top. Press the seam allowances toward the outer border.

Complete the Tray

1. Mat and frame the quilt top as desired. This quilt top was matted with dark green and white mats and mounted in an 18¾×30½" frame with glass. Spacers were added between the glass and the fabric to preserve the quilt.

2. Attach a screw-mounted drawer pull at each end of the frame for handles.

TEA COZY

Take comfort in the simple pleasure

of a pot full of tea kept warm under

a quilted tea cozy.

Materials

½ yard of pink-and-blue floral for blocks and

   cording cover

¼ yard of white print for blocks and border

¼ yard of pink toile for corner triangles

½ yard of backing fabric

2—18" squares of quilt batting

1¾ yards of ¼"-diameter cotton cording

24" of white single-fold bias tape

Finished block: 8" square

Cut the Fabrics

To make the best use of your fabrics, cut the pieces in the order that follows.

The corner triangles are cut slightly larger than necessary. They'll be trimmed to the correct size after they are sewn to the quilt blocks.

From pink-and-blue floral, cut:
- 1—4⅞" square, cutting it in half diagonally for a total of 2 large triangles
- 6—2⅞" squares, cutting each in half diagonally for a total of 12 small triangles
- 1—18" square, cutting it into enough 1½" wide bias strips to total 60" in length, for cording cover (For specific instructions on cutting bias strips, see Quilter's Schoolhouse, which begins on *page 145.*)

From white print, cut:
- 1—4⅞" square, cutting it in half diagonally for a total of 2 large triangles
- 6—2⅞" squares, cutting each in half diagonally for a total of 12 small triangles
- 12—2½" squares

From pink toile print, cut:
- 4—6¾" squares, cutting each in half diagonally for a total of 8 corner triangles

Assemble the Cake Stand Blocks

Referring to the Assemble the Cake Stand Blocks instructions on *page 72,* use six pink-and-blue floral small triangles, six white print small triangles, one pink-and-blue floral large triangle, one white print large triangle, and six white print 2½" squares to make a Cake Stand block. Repeat to make a total of two Cake Stand blocks.

Assemble the Block Surround

1. Sew a pink toile corner triangle to one edge of a Cake Stand block. Add a second pink toile corner triangle to the opposite edge. Then sew pink toile corner triangles to the remaining raw edges of the Cake Stand block to make a quilt top. Press all seam allowances toward the pink toile corner triangles. Repeat with the second Cake Stand block to make a second quilt top.

2. Trim the corner triangles to square up the quilt tops, leaving a ¼" seam allowance beyond the Cake Stand block corners. The pieced quilt tops should measure 11⅞" square, including the seam allowances.

Complete the Tea Cozy

1. Layer each quilt top with batting and backing according to the instructions in Quilter's Schoolhouse, which begins on *page 145*. Quilt as desired.

2. The tea cozy pattern is on *Pattern Sheet 2*. To make a template of the pattern, follow the instructions in Quilter's Schoolhouse.

From *each* quilt top, cut:
• 1 of Tea Cozy Pattern

3. Using the pink-and-blue floral bias strips and the cording, create 60" of covered cording (see Quilter's Schoolhouse for instructions).

From the covered cording, cut:
• 1—28½"-long piece
• 1—24½"-long piece
• 1—7"-long piece

4. Aligning the raw edges, pin the 28½"-long covered cording piece along the sides and top of one tea cozy piece; sew together.

5. Turn the long edge of the 7"-long covered cording piece under ¼" and slip-stitch the folded edge in place to conceal the raw edge. Fold the covered cording in half to make a corded loop. With raw edges aligned, pin the corded loop to the center top edge of the corded tea cozy piece to make the tea cozy front (see Assembly Diagram).

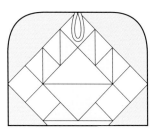

Assembly Diagram

6. Sew together the tea cozy front and the second tea cozy piece with the cording seam allowance and loop between layers to create the tea cozy. Turn right side out.

7. Aligning the raw edges of the 24½"-long cording piece with the raw edge of the tea cozy bottom, pin the covered cording to the tea cozy. Starting at one side of the tea cozy, stitch the cording to the right side of the tea cozy, beginning 1½" from the covered cording's folded end.

8. Once the covered cording is stitched around the edge of the tea cozy, cut the end of the cording so that it fits snugly into the folded opening at the beginning. The ends of the cording should abut inside the cording cover. Stitch the ends down and trim the raw edges as needed.

9. Aligning the raw edges of the bias tape with the tea cozy's seam allowance, sew together. Turn the bias tape to the inside and slip-stitch in place to cover the unfinished edge.

Colorful Creations

SIGNATURE QUILT

To commemorate a special occasion, create a signature quilt to use in place of a traditional guest book. Long after the party is over, this quilt will serve as a reminder of that special day.

Materials

½ yard total of assorted light prints for blocks

¼ yard total of assorted red prints for blocks

⅜ yard of red-and-black floral for setting and corner triangles

½ yard of black-and-red print for inner border and binding

⅜ yard of red-and-black print for outer border

1 yard of backing fabric

36" square of quilt batting

Permanent fine-line fabric pen

Finished quilt top: 29¾" square
Finished block: 8" square

Cut the Fabrics

To make the best use of your fabrics, cut the pieces in the order that follows. The setting and corner triangles are cut slightly larger than necessary. You'll trim them to the correct size after piecing the quilt center.

From assorted light prints, cut:
- 3—4⅞" squares, cutting each in half diagonally for a total of 6 large triangles (there will be 1 left over)
- 15—2⅞" squares, cutting each in half diagonally for a total of 30 small triangles
- 30—2½" squares

From assorted red prints, cut:
- 3—4⅞" squares, cutting each in half diagonally for a total of 6 large triangles (there will be 1 left over)
- 15—2⅞" squares, cutting each in half diagonally for a total of 30 small triangles

From red-and-black floral, cut:
- 1—12¾" square, cutting it diagonally twice in an X for a total of 4 setting triangles
- 2—6¾" squares, cutting each in half diagonally for a total of 4 corner triangles

From black-and-red print, cut:
- 4—1¼×25" inner border strips
- 4—2½×42" binding strips

From red-and-black print, cut:
- 4—3¼×31" outer border strips

Assemble the Cake Stand Blocks

Referring to the Assemble the Cake Stand Blocks instructions on *page 72,* use six light print small triangles, six red print small triangles, one light print large triangle, one red print large triangle, and six light print 2½" squares to make a Cake Stand block. Repeat to make a total of five Cake Stand blocks.

Assemble the Quilt Top

1. Referring to the photograph at *right,* lay out the five Cake Stand blocks and four red-and-black floral setting triangles in diagonal rows.

2. Sew together the pieces in each diagonal row. Press the seam allowances in one direction, alternating the direction with each row. Then join the rows. Press the seam allowances in one direction. Add the red-and-black floral print corner triangles to make the quilt center. Press the seam allowances toward the corner triangles.

3. Trim the setting and corner triangles to square up the quilt center, leaving a ¼" seam allowance beyond the corners of the Cake Stand blocks. The pieced quilt center should measure 23¼" square, including the seam allowances.

4. Center and sew a black-and-red print inner border strip to a red-and-black print outer border strip to

make a border strip set. Repeat to make a total of four border strip sets.

5. With midpoints aligned, join the border strip sets to the pieced quilt center, mitering the corners to complete the quilt top. For information on mitering, see the Mitered Border Corner instructions in Quilter's Schoolhouse, which begins on *page 145.*

Complete the Quilt

1. Layer the quilt top, batting, and backing according to the directions in Quilter's Schoolhouse.

2. Quilt as desired. The blocks in this quilt were machine-quilted in the ditch. The setting triangles and the borders were quilted following the fabric print.

3. Use the black-and-red print 2½×42" strips to bind the quilt according to the directions in Quilter's Schoolhouse.

4. Use the permanent fine-line fabric pen to sign the blocks as desired.

DURANGO
Pinwheel

To set off a palette of bright fabrics, quilt designer Jackie Robinson

chose a solid black fabric for her background. The resulting sparkly

twin-bed-size quilt appears to be filled with brilliant twirling pinwheels.

Materials

24—9×22" pieces (fat eighths) of assorted bright
   prints for blocks

⅝ yard of solid magenta for pinwheels and border

4½ yards of solid black for blocks, borders,
   and binding

3¾ yards of backing fabric

65×80" of quilt batting

Finished quilt top: 59×74"
Finished block: 7½" square

Quantities specified for 44/45"-wide, 100% cotton
fabrics. All measurements include a ¼" seam
allowance. Sew with right sides together unless
otherwise stated.

continued

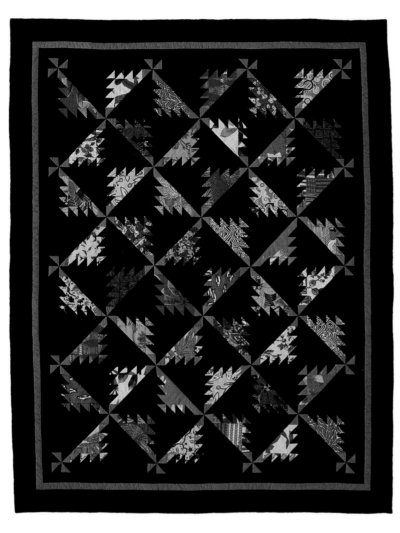

From solid black, cut:

- 7—2½×42" binding strips
- 2—3½×68½" outer border strips
- 2—3½×59½" outer border strips
- 2—2×63½" inner border strips
- 2—2×51½" inner border strips
- 14—2×12½" strips for pieced border
- 24—8⅜" squares, cutting each in half diagonally for a total of 48 large triangles
- 184—2⅜" squares, cutting each in half diagonally for a total of 368 small triangles

Assemble the Triangle-Squares

1. Sew together one bright print small triangle and one solid black small triangle to make a triangle-square (see Diagram 1). Press the seam allowance toward the solid black triangle. The pieced triangle-square should measure 2" square, including the seam allowances.

Diagram 1

2. Repeat Step 1 to make a total of 336 black-and-bright-print triangle-squares. In the same manner, make 32 black-and-magenta triangle-squares, which will be used in the border.

Piece the Blocks

1. For one block, you'll need seven matching black-and-bright-print triangle-squares, two solid magenta triangles, one bright print large triangle, and one solid black large triangle.

2. Referring to Diagram 2, sew together three triangle-squares and one solid magenta triangle in a horizontal row. Press the seam allowances in one direction. Add the unit to the bright print large triangle. Press the seam allowance toward the bright print large triangle.

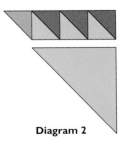

Diagram 2

Cut the Fabrics

To make the best use of your fabrics, cut the pieces in the order that follows. Cut the border strips the length of the fabric (parallel to the selvage). The border strip measurements are mathematically correct. You may wish to cut your border strips longer than specified to allow for possible sewing differences.

From *each* of 24 assorted bright prints, cut:

- 1—5⅜" square, cutting it in half diagonally for a total of 2 large triangles
- 7—2⅜" squares, cutting each in half diagonally for a total of 14 small triangles

From solid magenta, cut:

- 6—1½×42" strips for middle border
- 64—2⅜" squares, cutting each in half diagonally for a total of 128 triangles

3. Referring to Diagram 3 for placement, sew together four triangle-squares and one solid magenta triangle in a vertical row. Press the seam allowances in one direction. Add the unit to the bright print large triangle. Press the seam allowance toward the bright print large triangle.

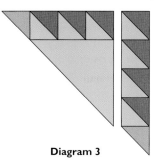

Diagram 3

4. Sew together the solid black large triangle and the Step 3 pieced triangle to complete a block (see Diagram 4). Press the seam allowance toward the solid black triangle. The pieced block should measure 8" square, including the seam allowances.

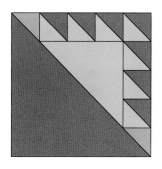

Diagram 4

5. Repeat steps 1 through 4 to make a total of 48 blocks.

Assemble the Quilt Center

Referring to the photograph *opposite* for placement, lay out the 48 blocks in eight horizontal rows. Sew together the blocks in each row. Press the seam allowances in one direction, alternating the direction with each row. Join the rows to make the quilt center. Press the seam allowances in one direction. The pieced quilt center should measure 45½×60½", including the seam allowances.

Assemble and Add the Pieced Border

1. Referring to Diagram 5 for placement, sew together three solid black 2×12½" strips and six black-and-magenta triangle-squares to make the pieced top border strip. Press the seam allowances toward the black strips. The pieced top border strip should measure 2×45½", including the seam allowances. Repeat to make a matching pieced bottom border strip.

2. Referring to the photograph *opposite* for placement, join the pieced border strips to the top and bottom edges of the pieced quilt center.

3. Referring to Diagram 6 for placement, sew together four solid black 2×12½" strips and 10 black-and-magenta triangle-squares to make a pieced side border strip. Press the seam allowances toward the black strips. The pieced side border strip should measure 2×63½", including the seam allowances. Repeat to make a second pieced side border strip.

4. Join the pieced side border strips to the side edges of the pieced quilt center. Press the seam allowances toward the border strips. The pieced quilt center should now measure 48½×63½".

Add the Remaining Borders

1. Sew a solid black 2×63½" inner border strip to each side edge of the pieced quilt center. Join a solid black 2×51½" inner border strip to the top and bottom edges of the pieced quilt center. Press all seam allowances toward the solid black border. The pieced quilt center should now measure 51½×66½", including seam allowances.

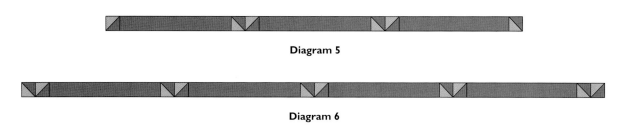

Diagram 5

Diagram 6

continued

2. Cut and piece the solid magenta 1½×42" strips to make:
- 2—1½×66½" middle border strips
- 2—1½×53½" middle border strips

3. Sew a long solid magenta border strip to each side edge of the pieced quilt center. Join a short solid magenta middle border strip to the top and bottom edges of the pieced quilt center. Press all seam allowances toward the solid magenta border. The pieced quilt center should now measure 53½×68½", including the seam allowances.

4. Sew a solid black 3½×68½" outer border strip to each side edge of the pieced quilt center. Join a solid black 3½×59½" outer border strip to the top and bottom edges of the pieced quilt center to complete the quilt top. Press all seam allowances toward the solid black outer border.

Complete the Quilt

1. Layer the quilt top, batting, and backing according to the instructions in Quilter's Schoolhouse, which begins on *page 145*. Quilt as desired.

2. Use the solid black 2½×42" strips to bind the quilt according to the instructions in Quilter's Schoolhouse.

optional colors

Changing the colorway of this traditional pattern results in finished projects with quite different looks. Whether you choose the bright colors of the original quilt or follow quilt tester Laura Boehnke's lead and select spring pastels or country colors, this pattern offers many possibilities.

Durango Pinwheel Quilt
optional sizes

If you'd like to make the quilt in a size other than for a twin bed, use the information *below*.

Alternate quilt sizes	Wall	Full	Queen/King
Number of blocks	16	80	144
Number of blocks wide by long	4×4	8×10	12×12
Finished size	41" square	71×86"	101" square
Yardage requirements			
9×22" pieces (fat eighths) of assorted bright prints	8	40	72
Solid magenta	½ yard	1¼ yards	1⅞ yards
Solid black	2¾ yards	5¾ yards	10¼ yards
Backing	2¾ yards	7 yards	9¼ yards
Batting	47" square	77×92"	107" square

QUILTED TABLECLOTH

Nostalgic fruit-print fabric combines with cheerful red and blue prints to create a simple table covering highlighted with a pieced edge.

Materials

- 1⅓ yards of 60"-wide white fruit print for tablecloth center
- ⅜ yard of solid white for border
- ⅜ yard total of assorted red and blue prints for border
- ⅜ yard of blue polka dot for binding
- 3 yards of backing fabric
- 54" square of quilt batting

Finished tablecloth: 48" square

Cut the Fabrics

To make the best use of your fabrics, cut the pieces in the order that follows.

From white fruit print, cut:
- 1—45½" square

From solid white, cut:
- 62—2⅜" squares, cutting each in half diagonally for a total of 124 triangles

From assorted red and blue prints, cut:
- 62—2⅜" squares, cutting each in half diagonally for a total of 124 triangles

From blue polka dot, cut:
- 5—2½×42" binding strips

Assemble the Triangle-Squares

Referring to the Assemble the Triangle-Squares instructions on *page 82*, use one solid white triangle and one red or blue print triangle to make a triangle-square. Repeat to make a total of 124 triangle-squares.

Assemble the Border

1. Sew together 30 triangle-squares in a row as shown in Diagram 1 on *page 86* to make a side border strip. Press the seam allowances in one direction. The side pieced border strip should measure 2×45½", including the seam allowances. Repeat to make a second side pieced border strip.

continued

2. Sew the pieced side border strips to opposite edges of the white fruit print 45½" square. Press the seam allowances toward the pieced borders.

3. Sew together 32 triangle-squares in a row as shown in Diagram 2 to make the top border strip. Note the direction of the triangle-squares on one end. Press the seam allowances in one direction. The pieced top border strip should measure 2×48½", including the seam allowances. Repeat to make a matching pieced bottom border strip.

4. Add the pieced border strips to the top and bottom edges of the quilt center to complete the quilt top. Press the seam allowances toward the pieced borders.

Complete the Tablecloth

1. Layer the quilt top, batting, and backing according to the instructions in Quilter's Schoolhouse, which begins on *page 145.* Quilt as desired.

2. Use the blue polka-dot 2½×42" strips to bind the quilt according to the instructions in Quilter's Schoolhouse.

Diagram 1

Diagram 2

CHAIR QUILT

Dress up an ordinary chair with a personal-size quilt that drapes over the back. Make a matching set for all your chairs, or, for a more individual look, rotate the color placement on each quilt to create one-of-a-kind seating for each of your guests.

Materials

18×22" piece (fat quarter) of white fruit print
  for blocks

18×22" piece (fat quarter) of red print for blocks

⅛ yard of blue print for binding

21" square of backing fabric

21" square of quilt batting

Finished quilt top: 15" square
Finished block: 7½" square

Cut the Fabrics

To make the best use of your fabrics, cut the pieces in the order that follows.

From white fruit print, cut:
- 2—8⅜" squares, cutting each in half diagonally for a total of 4 large triangles
- 18—2⅜" squares, cutting each in half diagonally for a total of 36 small triangles

From red print, cut:
- 2—5⅜" squares, cutting each in half diagonally for a total of 4 large triangles
- 14—2⅜" squares, cutting each in half diagonally for a total of 28 small triangles

From blue print cut:
- 2—2×42" binding strips

Assemble the Triangle Squares

Referring to the Assemble the Triangle-Squares instructions on *page 82,* use one white fruit print small triangle and one red print small triangle to make a triangle-square. Repeat to make a total of 28 triangle-squares.

Assemble the Blocks

Referring to the Piece the Blocks instructions on *page 82* and the Block Assembly Diagram *above right,* use seven triangle squares, two small white fruit print triangles, one large red print triangle, and one large white fruit print triangle to make a block. Repeat to make a total of four blocks.

Assemble the Quilt Top

Referring to the photograph *above* for placement, lay out the four blocks in two horizontal rows.

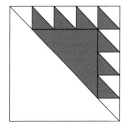

Block Assembly Diagram

Sew together the blocks in each row. Press the seam allowances in one direction, alternating the direction with each row. Join the rows to complete the quilt top. Press the seam allowance in one direction. The pieced quilt top should measure 15½" square, including the seam allowances.

Complete the Quilt

1. Layer the quilt top, batting, and backing according to the instructions in Quilter's Schoolhouse, which begins on *page 145.* Quilt as desired.

2. Use the blue print 2×42" binding strips to bind the quilt according to the instructions in Quilter's Schoolhouse.

BABY QUILT

Perfect in pastels, the pinwheels spin inside a scrappy border on this baby quilt. If you're making it for a toddler, use a variety of novelty prints.

Materials

1½ yards of light blue print for blocks, border, and binding

16—9×22" pieces (fat eighths) of assorted pastel prints for blocks and border

½ yard of pink print for blocks and border

2⅞ yards of backing fabric

50" square of quilt batting

Finished quilt top: 44" square
Finished block: 7½" square

Cut the Fabrics

To make the best use of your fabrics, cut the pieces in the order that follows. The border strip measurements are mathematically correct. You may wish to cut your border strips longer than specified to allow for possible sewing differences.

From blue print, cut:
- 5—2½×42" binding strips
- 2—2×36½" inner border strips
- 2—2×33½" inner border strips
- 8—2×12½" strips
- 8—8⅜" squares, cutting each in half diagonally for a total of 16 large triangles
- 66—2⅜" squares, cutting each in half diagonally for a total of 132 small triangles

From *each* of 16 assorted pastel prints, cut:
- 1—5⅜" square, cutting it in half diagonally for a total of two large triangles (there will be 1 left over from each pair)
- 4—2⅜" squares, cutting each in half diagonally for a total of 8 small triangles (there will be 1 left over from each set of 8)

From assorted pastel print scraps, cut:
- 50—3½" squares

From pink print, cut:
- 2—1½×38½" middle border strips
- 2—1½×36½" middle border strips
- 26—2⅜" squares, cutting each in half diagonally for a total of 52 small triangles

Assemble the Blocks

1. Referring to the Assemble the Triangle-Squares instructions on *page 82*, use the 16 sets of seven pastel print small triangles and 112 blue print small triangles to make a total of 112 pastel-and-blue triangle-squares. In the same manner, make a total of 20 pink-and-blue triangle squares.

2. Referring to the Piece the Blocks instructions on *page 82*, use one pastel print large triangle, seven matching pastel-and-blue triangle-squares, two pink print small triangles, and one blue print large triangle to make a block. Repeat to make a total of 16 blocks.

Assemble the Quilt Center

Referring to the photograph *opposite* for placement, lay out the 16 blocks in four horizontal rows. Sew together the blocks in each row. Press the seam allowances in one direction, alternating the direction

Colorful Creations

with each row. Join the rows to make the quilt center. Press the seam allowances in one direction. The pieced quilt center should measure 30½" square, including the seam allowances.

Assemble and Add the Pieced Inner Border

1. To make the pieced inner border you'll need eight blue print 2×12½" strips and 20 pink-and-blue triangle-squares.

2. Referring to the Assemble and Add the Pieced Border instructions on *page 83*, sew together two blue print 2×12½" strips and four pink-and-blue triangle-squares in a row to make a pieced side border strip. The pieced side border strip should measure 2×30½", including the seam allowances. Repeat to make a second pieced side border strip.

3. Join a pieced side border strip to each side edge of the pieced quilt center.

4. Referring to the Assemble and Add the Pieced Border instructions on *page 83*, sew together two 2×12½" strips and six pink-and-blue triangle-squares in a row to make a pieced top border strip. The pieced top border strip should measure 2×33½", including the seam allowances. Repeat to make a matching pieced bottom border strip.

5. Referring to the photograph *above* for placement, join the pieced border strips to the top and bottom edges of the pieced quilt center. Press all seam allowances toward the pieced border. The pieced quilt center should now measure 33½" square, including the seam allowances.

Add the Remaining Borders

1. Add a blue print 2×33½" inner border strip to each side edge of the pieced quilt center and a blue print 2×36½" inner border strip to the top and bottom edges of the pieced quilt center. Press the seam allowances toward the blue print border. The pieced quilt center should now measure 36½" square, including the seam allowances.

2. Sew a pink print 1½×36½" middle border strip to each side edge of the pieced quilt center and a pink print 1½×38½" middle border strip to the top and bottom edges of the pieced quilt

center. Press the seam allowances toward the pink print border. The pieced quilt center should now measure 38½" square, including the seam allowances.

3. Sew together the pastel print 3½" squares and trim to make the following:
- 2—3½×44½" outer border strips
- 2—3½×38½" outer border strips

4. Add a short pieced outer border strip to each side edge of the pieced quilt center and a long pieced outer border strip to the top and bottom edges of the pieced quilt center to complete the quilt top. Press the seam allowances toward the pink print border.

Complete the Quilt

1. Layer the quilt top, batting, and backing according to the instructions in Quilter's Schoolhouse, which begins on *page 145*. Quilt as desired.

2. Use the blue print 2½×42" strips to bind the quilt according to the instructions in Quilter's Schoolhouse.

STAR ATTRACTIONS

There may be no motif as prevalent in quilting as
the star. Appearing in all sizes and configurations,
stars have danced across the surface of quilts
since quilts were first pieced, and they have
resonated with us ever since. Whether created in
a classic two-color scheme or made in a mixture
of bright colors, stars remain a favorite design
choice of quilters and quilt lovers everywhere.

AMERICAN *Beauty*

An antique quilt inspired quiltmakers Joy Hoffman and Bonnie Erickson to

create this red-and-cream classic and coordinating throw pillows.

Materials

7 yards of cream print for blocks and border

4¾ yards of red print for blocks, border, and binding

7¾ yards of backing fabric

92×105" of quilt batting

Finished quilt top: 84¾×97½"

Quantities specified for 44/45"-wide, 100% cotton fabrics. All measurements include a ¼" seam allowance. Sew with right sides together unless otherwise stated.

Designer Notes

An antique quilt they saw at a quilt show inspired quiltmakers Joy Hoffman and Bonnie Erickson to create this red-and-cream bed-size project, though each was interested in making it for a different reason. Joy was attracted by the two-color patchwork while Bonnie wanted the open spaces for machine-quilting. The two combined their talents with stunning results.

Cut the Fabrics

To make the best use of your fabrics, cut the pieces in the order that follows. Cut the border strips the length of the fabric (parallel to the selvage). The border strip measurements are mathematically correct. You may wish to cut your border strips longer than specified to allow for possible sewing differences.

The patterns are on *Pattern Sheet 2.* To make templates of the patterns, follow the instructions in Quilter's Schoolhouse, which begins on *page 145.*

continued

From cream print, cut:
- 2—9×85¼" outer border strips
- 2—9×81" outer border strips
- 5—10" squares, cutting each diagonally twice in an X for a total of 20 side setting triangles (there will be 2 left over)
- 50—6½" squares for setting
- 2—5½" squares, cutting each in half diagonally for a total of 4 corner triangles
- 240 of Pattern A
- 262—2" squares

From red print, cut:
- 2—2½×77" inner border strips
- 2—2½×68¼" inner border strips
- 10—2½×42" binding strips
- 71—3½" squares
- 240 *each* of patterns B and B reversed

Assemble the Center and Edge Units

1. For accurate sewing lines, use a quilter's pencil to mark a diagonal line on the wrong side of the 262 cream print 2" squares. (To prevent your fabric from stretching as you draw the lines, place 220-grit sandpaper under the squares.)

2. Align a marked cream print 2" square with one corner of a red print 3½" square (see Diagram 1; note the placement of the diagonal line). Stitch on the marked line; trim the seam allowance to ¼". Press the attached triangle open. Align a second marked cream print 2" square with the opposite corner of the red print square; stitch, trim, and press as before. In the same manner, sew a marked cream print 2" square in the remaining corners of the red print square to make a center unit. The pieced center unit should measure 3½" square, including seam allowances. Repeat to make a total of 49 center units.

Diagram 1

3. Referring to Diagram 2, add three marked cream print 2" squares to a red print 3½" square as in Step 2 to make an edge unit; trim and press. The pieced edge unit should measure 3½" square, including the seam allowances. Repeat to make a total of 22 edge units.

Diagram 2

Assemble the Star Units

1. Referring to Diagram 3, join a red print B triangle, a cream print A triangle, and a red print B reversed triangle to make a star point unit. Press the seam allowances toward the red print triangles. The pieced star point unit should measure 3½" square, including the seam allowances. Repeat to make a total of 240 star point units.

Diagram 3

2. Sew together two star point units to make a star unit (see Diagram 4). Press the seam allowance in one direction. The pieced star unit should measure 3½×6½", including seam allowances. Repeat to make a total of 120 star units.

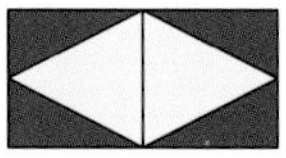

Diagram 4

Assemble the Quilt Center

1. Referring to the Quilt Assembly Diagram *opposite*, lay out the 49 center units, the 22 edge units, the 120 star units, the 50 cream print 6½" setting squares, and 18 cream print side setting triangles in diagonal rows.

2. Sew together the pieces in each diagonal row. Press the seam allowances toward the center units, cream print setting squares, and cream print setting triangles. Then join the rows. Press the seam allowances in one direction. Add the four cream print corner triangles to complete the quilt center. Press the seam allowances toward the corner triangles.

3. Trim the setting and corner triangles, leaving a ¼" seam allowance beyond the block corners. The pieced quilt center should measure 64¼×77", including seam allowances.

Add the Borders

1. Sew one red print 2½×77" inner border strip to each side edge of the pieced quilt center. Add a red print 2½×68¼" inner border strip to the top and bottom edges of the pieced quilt center. Press the seam allowances toward the red print border.

2. Sew one cream print 9×81" outer border strip to each side edge of the pieced quilt center. Add a cream print 9×85¼" outer border strip to the top and bottom edges of the pieced quilt center to complete the quilt top. Press all seam allowances toward the cream print border.

Complete the Quilt

1. Layer the quilt top, batting, and backing according to the instructions in Quilter's Schoolhouse, which begins on *page 145.*

2. Quilt as desired. Bonnie used cream-color thread to machine-quilt the setting squares and triangles with feather designs and surrounded them with heavy stippling.

3. Use the red print 2½×42" strips to bind the quilt according to the instructions in Quilter's Schoolhouse.

Quilt Assembly Diagram

American Beauty Quilt
optional sizes

If you'd like to make this quilt in a size other than for a full/queen-size bed, use the information *below.*

Alternate quilt sizes	Crib/Lap	Twin	King
Number of setting squares	8	18	72
Number of setting squares wide by long	2×3	3×4	6×7
Finished size	46½×59¼"	59¼×72"	97½×110¼"
Yardage requirements			
Cream print	2½ yards	3⅝ yards	9 yards
Red print	2¼ yards	3 yards	6½ yards
Backing	2⅓ yards	3⅔ yards	8⅔ yards
Batting	52×66"	66×78"	104×117"

DOUBLE RUFFLE PILLOW

The star from the "American Beauty" quilt takes center stage on this double-ruffle throw pillow, above right, *resulting in a charming bed ensemble accessory.*

Materials

½ yard of red print for block and ruffle

⅛ yard of solid cream for block

¼ yard of cream-and-red stripe for ruffle

½ yard of tan-and-red print for setting triangles and backing

12" pillow form

Finished pillow cover: 12" square (excluding ruffle)

Cut the Fabrics

To make the best use of your fabrics, cut the pieces in the order that follows. This project uses "American Beauty" patterns on *Pattern Sheet 2.* To make templates of the patterns, follow the instructions in Quilter's Schoolhouse, which begins on *page 145.*

From red print, cut:
- 3—4×42" strips
- 1—3½" square
- 4 *each* of patterns B and B reversed

From solid cream, cut:
- 4—3½" squares
- 4—2" squares
- 4 of Pattern A

From cream-and-red stripe, cut:
- 3—1¾×42" strips

From tan-and-red print, cut:
- 1—15" square
- 2—7½" squares, cutting each in half diagonally to make a total of 4 setting triangles

Assemble the Star Block

1. For accurate sewing lines, use a quilter's pencil to mark a diagonal line on the wrong side of the four solid cream 2" squares.

2. Referring to Assemble the Center and Edge Units, Step 2, on *page 94,* make one center unit.

3. Referring to Assemble the Star Units, Step 1, on *page 94,* make four star point units.

4. Referring to Diagram 1 for placement, lay out the center unit, the four star point units, and the four

solid cream 3½" squares in three horizontal rows. Sew together the pieces in each row. Press the seam allowances toward the solid cream squares and center unit. Then join the rows to complete a star block. Press the seam allowances in one direction. The pieced star block should measure 9½" square, including the seam allowances.

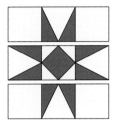

Diagram 1

Assemble the Pillow Top

1. Sew a tan-and-red print setting triangle to opposite edges of the pieced star block (see Diagram 2). Press the seam allowances toward the setting triangles.

Diagram 2

2. Then sew a tan-and-red print setting triangle to the remaining raw edges of the star block to complete the pillow top. Press the seam allowances toward the setting triangles. Trim the pieced pillow top to measure 13" square, including the seam allowances.

Make a Mock Double Ruffle

Making a mock double ruffle like the one shown on the pillow on *page 96* saves fabric and reduces bulk in the seams.

1. Cut and piece the cream-and-red stripe 1¾×42" strips to create a 1¾×120" strip. Cut and piece the red print 4×42" strips to create a 4×120" strip.

2. Layer the strips with right sides together and long edges aligned; sew together the aligned long edges. Press the seam allowance open.

3. Join the short ends of the layered strips to make a circle. Press the seam allowance open. Fold and press the circle in half lengthwise with wrong side inside (see Diagram 3). Machine-baste two rows approximately ³⁄₁₆" apart and close to the raw edges to make a mock double ruffle. Gather the ruffle to the desired fullness by gently pulling the threads.

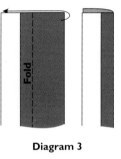

Diagram 3

4. Matching raw edges, layer the ruffle on the pillow top. Starting at the center of one side, pin the ruffle around the pillow top; adjust the fullness as you pin and allow extra fullness at the corners.

5. Baste the ruffle to the pillow top with a ½" seam allowance.

Complete the Pillow

1. Trim the tan-and-red print 15" square pillow back to the same size as the pillow top.

2. Place the pillow back atop the pillow top with right sides together. Sew together with a ½" seam allowance, leaving a 4–5" opening along one side. Diagonally trim the corners to remove bulk in the seam allowance. Turn the pillow cover right side out through the opening.

3. Using a blunt object, such as a crochet hook or the eraser end of a pencil, poke out the pillow corners. Push in the pillow form. Slip-stitch the opening closed.

SINGLE RUFFLE PILLOW

A solid center square and Four-Patch

corner units add a twist to this "American

Beauty" throw pillow, shown at left in the

photo on page 96.

Materials

⅛ yard of red print for block

⅛ yard of tan-and-red print for block

⅛ yard of cream-and-red print for block

⅛ yard of solid cream for block

¾ yard of cream-and-red stripe for ruffle and backing

9" pillow form

Finished pillow cover: 9" square (excluding ruffle)

Cut the Fabrics

To make the best use of your fabrics, cut the pieces in the order that follows. This project uses "American Beauty" patterns on *Pattern Sheet 2*. To make templates of the patterns, follow the instructions in Quilter's Schoolhouse, which begins on *page 145*.

From red print, cut:
• 4 of Pattern A
• 1—3½" square
• 8—2" squares

From tan-and-red print, cut:
• 4—2" squares

From cream-and-red print, cut:
• 4—2" squares

From solid cream, cut:
• 4 *each* of patterns B and B reversed

From cream-and-red stripe, cut:
• 1—12" square
• 3—4½×42" strips for ruffle

Assemble the Star Block

1. Referring to Assemble the Star Units, Step 1, on *page 94*, make four star point units.

2. Referring to Diagram 1, lay out two red print 2" squares and two tan-and-red print 2" squares in two rows.

Diagram I

Sew together the squares in each row. Press the seam allowances in opposite directions. Then join the rows to complete a Four-Patch unit. Press the seam allowance in one direction. The pieced Four-Patch unit should measure 3½" square, including the seam allowances. Repeat to make a matching Four-Patch unit.

3. Repeat Step 2, substituting the cream-and-red print 2" squares for the tan-and-red print 2" squares, to make two more Four-Patch units.

4. Referring to Diagram 2, lay out the four star point units, the four Four-Patch units, and the red print 3½" square in three horizontal rows. Sew together the pieces in each row. Press the seam allowances

Diagram 2

toward the Four-Patch units and red print 3½" square. Then join the rows to complete a star block. Press the seam allowances in one direction. The pieced star block should measure 9½" square, including the seam allowances.

Make a Single Ruffle

1. Cut and piece the cream-and-red stripe 4½×42" strips to create a 4½×100" strip, which includes a ¼" seam allowance.

2. Referring to Make a Mock Double Ruffle, steps 3 through 5, on *page 97*, assemble and gather a single ruffle, and baste it to the pillow top with a ¼" seam allowance.

Complete the Pillow

Referring to the Complete the Pillow instructions on *page 97*, use a ¼" seam allowance to finish the pillow.

Star Attractions

APPLIQUÉ JACKET

No-fray faux suede is the perfect fabric

choice for this quick-and-easy star appliqué.

Materials

4" square of light blue Ultrasuede

2½×5" square of black Ultrasuede

3×5" piece each of purple, red, yellow,

    and green Ultrasuede

¼ yard of fusing-adhesive material (we used

    Steam-A-Seam 2)

Denim jacket

Cut the Fabrics

To make the best use of your fabrics, cut the pieces in the order that follows. This project uses "American Beauty" Pattern B, which is on *Pattern Sheet 2*. To make a template of the pattern, follow the instructions in Quilter's Schoolhouse, which begins on *page 145*. *Note:* For this project, we made a template following the solid cutting lines on Pattern B, extending the longest lines to a point to make a triangle.

1. Lay the fusing-adhesive material, paper side up, over Pattern B. With a pencil, trace Pattern B four times and Pattern B reversed four times, leaving ½" between tracings. Cut out, cutting about ¼" outside of the traced lines.

2. In the same manner, cut one 3½" square and two 2½" squares from fusing-adhesive material.

3. Following the manufacturer's instructions, press the fusing-adhesive material pieces onto the backs of the Ultrasuede scraps as indicated *above*. Then cut out the Ultrasuede pieces and peel off the paper backings.

From light blue, cut:
- 1—3⅛" square

From black, cut:
- 2—2¼" squares, cutting each in half diagonally for a total of 4 triangles

From purple, red, yellow, and green, cut:
- 1 *each* of patterns B and B reversed

Appliqué the Jacket

1. Referring to the photograph *above* for placement, lay out the light blue 3⅛" square, the four black triangles, and the eight assorted B and B reversed triangles on the center back of the denim jacket.

2. When the appliqué pieces are positioned where you want them, cover them with a pressing cloth and fuse them into place following the manufacturer's instructions; let the fabrics cool. Check to be sure all the appliqué points are securely adhered; repeat fusing if necessary to secure all edges.

SHOWER CURTAIN

Quilts can go beyond the living room and bedroom. A border of blocks from the "American Beauty" quilt forms the focal point of this quilted shower curtain. Size this project to fit your tub opening by adjusting the number of blocks in the border.

Materials

⅝ yard of green print for blocks

8—9×22" pieces (fat eighths) of assorted cream and tan prints for blocks

¼ yard total of assorted rust prints for blocks

2¼ yards of cream print for border

⅓ yard of solid rust for border

2¼ yards of rust-and-green stripe for curtain

1¼ yards of rust floral print for curtain

4⅓ yards of lining fabric

1¼ yards of backing fabric

21×89" of quilt batting

Finished shower curtain: 82×72¾"
Finished star block: 9" square

Cut the Fabrics

To make the best use of your fabrics, cut the pieces in the order that follows. This project uses "American Beauty" patterns, which are on *Pattern Sheet 2*. To make templates of the patterns, follow the instructions in Quilter's Schoolhouse, which begins on *page 145*.

Cut the cream print border strips the length of the fabric (parallel to the selvage). The border strip measurements are mathematically correct. You may wish to cut your border strips longer than specified to allow for possible sewing differences.

From green print, cut:
- 32 of Pattern A
- 8—3½" squares
- 64—2" squares

From *each* of the 8 assorted cream and tan prints, cut:
- 4 *each* of patterns B and B reversed

From assorted rust prints, cut:
- 64—2" squares

From cream print, cut:
- 2—17×5½" border strips
- 2—4¼×72½" border strips

From solid rust, cut:
- 6—1½×42" strips for border

From rust-and-green stripe, cut
- 2—37½×42" rectangles

From rust floral, cut:
- 2—19½×42" rectangles

From lining, cut:
- 2—73½×42" rectangles

Assemble the Star Blocks

1. Referring to Assemble the Star Units, Step 1, on *page 94*, make a total of 32 star point units.

2. Referring to Assemble the Star Block on *page 98*, Step 2, use the the green print 2" squares and the rust print 2" squares to make a total of 32 Four-Patch units.

3. Referring to Assemble the Star Block on *page 98*, Step 4, use four star point units, four Four-Patch units and a green print 3½" square to make a star block. Repeat to make a total of eight star blocks.

Assemble the Star Border

1. Sew together the eight Star blocks in a horizontal row. Press the seam allowances in one direction. The pieced block row should measure 9½×72½", including the seam allowances.

2. Join a cream print 4¼×72½" strip to the top and bottom edges of the pieced block row. Press the seam allowances toward the cream print strips.

Then sew a cream print 17×5½" strip to each side edge of the pieced block row to complete the block border. Press the seam allowances toward the cream print strips. The pieced star block border should measure 17×82½", including the seam allowances.

Quilt the Border

Layer the star block border, batting, and backing according to the instructions in Quilter's Schoolhouse, which begins on *page 145*. Quilt as desired. Trim the quilted border to measure 16½×82½", including the seam allowances.

Assemble the Shower Curtain

1. Cut and piece the solid rust 1½×42" strips to make the following:
   - 3—1½×82½" border strips

2. Cut and piece the rust-and-green stripe 37½×42" rectangles to make the following:
   - 1—82½×37½" rectangle

3. Cut and piece the rust floral 19½×42" rectangles to make the following:
   - 1—82½×19½" rectangle

4. Cut and piece the 73½×42" lining rectangles to make the following:
   - 1—82½×73½" rectangle

5. Referring to the photograph at *right* for placement, sew a solid rust 1½×82½" strip to the top edges of the star border, the rust-and-green stripe 82½×37½" rectangle, and the rust floral 82½×19½" rectangle. Then join the three sections to make the shower curtain.

6. Turn under the shower curtain's lower edge ¼" and press. Then fold it under 2" to make a hem. Topstitch the hem in place.

7. In the same manner, turn under the lining 82½×73½" rectangle's lower edge; topstitch the hem in place.

8. With right sides together, sew the shower curtain to the lining at the side and top edges, leaving the hemmed bottom edges free. Turn right side out and press. From the front of the shower curtain, edge-stitch along the top and side edges.

9. Using lining fabric, sew a hanging sleeve to the lining's top edge according to the instructions in Quilter's Schoolhouse. (*Note:* Hang a second shower curtain rod with a waterproof liner behind the quilted shower curtain to prevent the fabric from getting wet.)

AUNT MAGGIE'S
Quilt

At first glance, it may appear that this quilt is composed of one repeated block.

But a closer examination reveals that project designer Darlene Zimmerman

produced that effect by surrounding 63 star blocks with sashing

to form an additional 48 blocks.

Materials

4⅓ yards of muslin for background

26—¼-yard pieces of assorted reproduction
   1930s prints for blocks

1 yard of lavender reproduction 1930s print for
   inner border, border corner squares, and binding

3⅞ yards of backing fabric

68×84" of quilt batting

Finished quilt top: 62×78"
Finished block: 6" square

Quantities specified for 44/45"-wide, 100% cotton
fabrics. All measurements include a ¼" seam
allowance. Sew with right sides together unless
otherwise stated.

Cut the Fabrics

To make the best use of your fabrics, cut the pieces
in the order that follows. The patterns are on *Pattern
Sheet 2.* To make templates of the patterns, follow
the instructions in Quilter's Schoolhouse, which
begins on *page 145.*

From muslin, cut:
- 28—2½×4½" rectangles *or* 28 of Pattern E
- 334—2½" squares *or* 334 of Pattern D
- 448 *each* of patterns A and A reversed
- 124 of Pattern B
- 132 of Pattern C

From *each* assorted print, cut:
- 22 of Pattern B
- 22 of Pattern C

From lavender print, cut:
- 7—2½×42" binding strips
- 7—1½×42" strips for inner border
- 4—3½" squares for border corners

continued

Assemble the Star Blocks

1. For one star block you'll need four muslin A triangles, four muslin A reversed triangles, four muslin D squares, two B triangles and two C triangles from one print, and two B triangles and two C triangles from a second print.

2. Sew together one muslin A triangle, one muslin A reversed triangle, and one print B triangle to make a star point unit (see Diagram 1). Press the seam allowances toward the B triangle. The pieced star point unit should measure 2½" square, including the seam allowances. Repeat with the remaining A and B triangles to make a total of four star point units.

Diagram 1

3. Sew together the four print C triangles in pairs as shown in Diagram 2. Press the seam allowances open. Then join the pairs to make a star center unit. Press the seam allowances open. The pieced star center unit should measure 2½" square, including the seam allowances.

Diagram 2

4. Lay out the four star point units, the star center unit, and four muslin D squares as shown in Diagram 3. Sew together the squares in each row. Press the seam allowances in one direction, alternating the direction with each row. Then join the rows to make a star block. Press the seam allowances in one direction. The pieced star block should measure 6½" square, including the seam allowances.

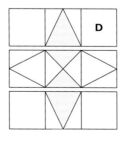

Diagram 3

5. Repeat steps 1 through 4 to make a total of 63 star blocks.

Assemble the Sashing Units

1. For one set of sashing units you'll need four muslin A triangles, four muslin A reversed triangles, two B triangles and two C triangles from one print, and two B triangles and two C triangles from a second print.

2. Referring to steps 2 and 3 under Assemble the Star Blocks *left*, sew together the pieces to make four star point units and one star center unit. Set aside a pair of matching star point units (see Diagram 4). Sew the other matching star point units to opposite sides of the star center unit to make a pieced sashing rectangle (see Diagram 5). The pieced sashing rectangle should measure 2½×6½", including the seam allowances.

Diagram 4   **Diagram 5**

3. Repeat steps 1 and 2 to make a total of 48 sets of one sashing rectangle and two star point units.

Assemble the Quilt Center

Referring to the Quilt Assembly Diagram, lay out the 63 star blocks in nine horizontal rows, leaving space between the blocks for the sashing units. Add the 48 pieced sashing rectangles, the matching star point units, the remaining 82 muslin D squares, and the muslin E rectangles between the star blocks. Lay out the entire quilt center before beginning the assembly to assure the sashing units are arranged correctly.

Once you're satisfied with your layout, sew together the pieces in each row. Press the seam allowances in one direction, alternating the direction with each row. Then join the rows to complete the quilt center. Press the seam allowances in one direction. The pieced quilt center should measure 54½×70½", including the seam allowances.

Assemble and Add the Borders

1. Cut and piece the lavender print 1½×42" strips to make the following:
- 2—1½×70½" inner border strips
- 2—1½×56½" inner border strips

2. Sew a long inner border strip to each side edge of the pieced quilt center. Then sew a short inner border strip to the top and bottom edges of the pieced quilt center. Press the seam allowances toward the lavender print border.

3. To make a pieced border unit you'll need 28 sets of matching print B and C triangles, 27 muslin B triangles, 29 muslin C triangles, one muslin A triangle, and one muslin A reversed triangle.

4. Referring to Diagram 6, lay out the B triangles in a row, alternating the fabrics, with the A and the A reversed triangles at the ends of the row. Join the triangles. Press the seam allowances toward the print triangles.

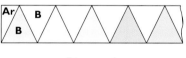

Diagram 6

5. Referring to Diagram 7, lay out the C triangles, placing the prints in the same order as was used with the B triangles in Step 4. Join the triangles. Press seam allowances toward the print triangles.

Diagram 7

6. Aligning the long raw edges and matching the seams, sew the pieced row from Step 4 to the top edge of the pieced row from Step 5 to create a pieced border unit. Trim the excess muslin C triangles at each end. Sew the pieced border strip to the top edge of the pieced quilt center.

7. Repeat steps 3 through 6 to make a second pieced border unit and add it to the bottom edge of the pieced quilt center.

8. To make a side border unit you'll need 36 sets of matching print B and C triangles, 35 muslin B triangles, 37 muslin C triangles, one muslin A triangle, one muslin A reversed triangle, and two lavender print 3½" squares.

9. In the same manner as for the top and bottom pieced border units, join the triangles for a side

Quilt Assembly Diagram

border unit in rows. Sew a lavender print 3½" square to each end of the pieced row. Join a pieced side border unit to each side edge of the pieced quilt center to complete the quilt top.

Complete the Quilt

1. Layer the quilt top, batting, and backing according to the instructions in Quilter's Schoolhouse, which begins on *page 145*.

2. Quilt as desired. Darlene Zimmerman hand-quilted ¼" from the star blocks' and border units' seam allowances. She used a shell design to fill the empty spaces along the edges of the quilt center.

3. Use the lavender print 2½×42" binding strips to bind the quilt according to the instructions in Quilter's Schoolhouse.

continued

Aunt Maggie's Quilt
optional sizes

If you'd like to make this quilt in a size other than given, use the information *below.*

Alternate quilt sizes	Crib/Lap	Full/Queen	King
Number of blocks	30	110	169
Number of blocks wide by long	5×6	10×11	13×13
Finished size	46×54"	86×94"	110" square
Yardage requirements			
Muslin	2¾ yards	8 yards	11 yards
Number of pieces of assorted prints	20–¼ yard	30–¼ yard	35–¼ yard
Lavender print	⅞ yard	1¼ yards	1½ yards
Backing	2⅞ yards	7⅔ yards	9⅔ yards
Batting	52×60"	92×100"	116" square

CHRISTMAS TREE SKIRT

Showcase your holiday tree with an elegant eight-point tree skirt.

Materials

2 yards of light gold print for blocks

13—⅛-yard pieces *each* of assorted red and green holiday prints for blocks

1 yard of dark gold print for blocks and border

¼ yard of dark green print for border

1¾ yards of red print for borders and binding

3⅞ yards of backing fabric

69" square of quilt batting

Finished quilt top: 62¼" square (point to point)
Finished block: 6" square

Cut the Fabrics

To make the best use of your fabrics, cut the pieces in the order that follows. This project uses "Aunt Maggie's Quilt" patterns on *Pattern Sheet 2.* To make templates of the patterns, follow the instructions in Quilter's Schoolhouse, which begins on *page 145.*

The border strip measurements are mathematically correct. You may wish to cut your border strips longer than specified to allow for possible sewing differences.

From light gold print, cut:

- 16—2½×4½" rectangles *or* 16 of Pattern E
- 124—2½" squares *or* 124 of Pattern D
- 164 *each* of patterns A and A reversed

From assorted red holiday prints, cut:

- 106 of Pattern B (53 sets of two matching)
- 106 of Pattern C (53 sets of two matching)

From assorted green holiday prints, cut:

- 106 of Pattern B (53 sets of two matching)
- 106 of Pattern C (53 sets of two matching)

From dark gold print, cut:

- 2—1½×40½" inner border strips
- 2—1½×38½" inner border strips
- 8 *each* of patterns A and A reversed
- 40 of Pattern B
- 48 of Pattern C
- 8 of Pattern F

From dark green print, cut:

- 5—1½×42" strips for middle border

From red print, cut:

- 4—3½" squares
- 5—1½×42" strips for outer border
- 2—10⅞" squares, cutting each in half diagonally for a total of 4 border setting triangles
- 1—27" square, cutting it into enough 2"-wide bias strips to total 270" in length for binding (For specific instructions on cutting bias strips, see Quilter's Schoolhouse, which begins on *page 145*.)

Assemble the Star Blocks

Referring to the Assemble the Star Blocks instructions on *page 104*, use four light gold print A triangles, four light gold print A reversed triangles, four light gold print D squares, two B triangles and two C triangles from one print, and two B triangles and two C triangles from a second print to make a star block. Repeat to make a total of 25 star blocks.

Assemble the Sashing Units

1. Referring to the Assemble the Sashing Units instructions on *page 104*, use four light gold print A triangles, four light gold print A reversed triangles, two B triangles and two C triangles from one red print, and two B triangles and two C triangles from one green print to make a set of one sashing rectangle and two star point units.

2. Repeat to make a total of 16 sets of one sashing rectangle and two star point units.

Assemble the Quilt Center

Referring to the Quilt Assembly Diagram on *page 108*, lay out the 25 star blocks in five horizontal rows, leaving space between the blocks for the sashing units. Add the 16 pieced sashing rectangles, the matching star point units, the remaining 24 light gold print D squares, and the light gold print E rectangles between the star blocks. Lay out the entire quilt center before beginning the assembly to assure the sashing units are arranged correctly.

Once you're satisfied with your layout, sew together the pieces in each row. Then join the rows to complete the quilt center. The pieced quilt center should measure 38½" square, including the seam allowances.

Add the First Set of Borders

1. Sew a dark gold print 1½×38½" inner border strip to opposite edges of the pieced quilt center. Then add a dark gold print 1½×40½" inner border strip to the remaining edges of the pieced quilt center. Press all seam allowances toward the dark gold print border.

2. Cut and piece the dark green 1½×42" strips to make the following:
   - 2—1½×42½" middle border strips
   - 2—1½×40½" middle border strips

3. Join a dark green print 1½×40½" middle border strip to opposite edges of the pieced quilt center. Then add a dark green print 1½×42½" middle border strip to the remaining edges of the pieced quilt center. Press all seam allowances toward the green print border.

continued

Quilt Assembly Diagram

4. Cut and piece the red print 1½×42" strips to make the following:
   - 2—1½×44½" outer border strips
   - 2—1½×42½" outer border strips

5. Sew a red print 1½×42½" outer border strip to opposite edges of the pieced quilt center. Then add a red print 1½×44½" outer border strip to the remaining edges of the pieced quilt center. Press all seam allowances toward the red print border. The pieced quilt center should measure 44½" square, including the seam allowances.

Assemble the Pieced Border

1. Referring to the Assemble and Add the Borders instructions, steps 3 through 6, on *page 105* and the lower border unit on Diagram 1 *below*, use

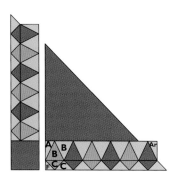

Diagram 1

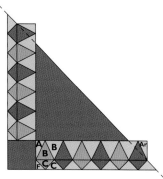

Diagram 2

three sets of matching red print B and C triangles, three sets of matching green print B and C triangles, five dark gold print B triangles, six dark gold print C triangles, one dark gold F triangle, one dark gold print A triangle, and one dark gold print A reversed triangle to make a pieced border unit. Repeat to make a total of four matching pieced border units.

2. In the same manner, referring to the left side border unit in Diagram 1 *below,* make a total of four mirror-image pieced border units.

Assemble the Border Corners

1. Referring to Diagram 1, join a pieced border unit to one short side of a red print border setting triangle. Sew a red print 3½" square to one end of a second pieced border unit. Then join that pieced border unit to the remaining short side of the red print border setting triangle.

2. Referring to Diagram 2, trim the pieced strip ends even with the raw edge of the red print setting triangle to make a pieced border corner. Repeat to make a total of four pieced border corners.

3. Fold and mark the center of a pieced border corner on the red print raw edge. Mark the center of one edge of the pieced quilt center. Matching the center marks, sew the pieced border corner to the pieced quilt center. Add the remaining pieced border corners to the quilt center in the same manner to complete the quilt top.

Complete the Tree Skirt

1. Layer the quilt top, batting, and backing according to the instructions in Quilter's Schoolhouse, which begins on *page 145.*

2. Quilt as desired. This tree skirt was machine-quilted with gold metallic thread.

3. Referring to the photograph on *page 106* for location, cut a straight slit to the quilt center. Cut a 3"- to 5"-diameter circle in the center of the quilt to allow space for a tree trunk.

4. Use the red print 2"-wide bias strips to bind the tree skirt, including both sides of the slit and around the inner circle, according to the instructions in Quilter's Schoolhouse.

TRAVEL BAG

Keep your blow dryer, hairbrushes, and other toiletries neatly stored in this dapper drawstring bag when you're on the go.

Materials

Scraps of gold print for border

Scraps of dark green solid for border

⅛ yard of yellow stripe for border

½ yard of dark green stripe for travel bag

1¼ yards of ¼"-diameter cording for drawstring

Finished travel bag: 12×17"
Finished border strip: 3×24"

Cut the Fabrics

To make the best use of your fabrics, cut the pieces in the order that follows. This project uses "Aunt Maggie's Quilt" Pattern C, which is on *Pattern Sheet 2*. The border strip measurements are mathematically correct. You may wish to cut your border strips longer than specified to allow for possible sewing differences.

From scraps of gold print, cut:
• 24 of Pattern C

From scraps of solid dark green, cut:
• 24 of Pattern C

From yellow stripe, cut:
• 2—1×24½" strips

From dark green stripe, cut:
• 1—11×24½" rectangle
• 1—4½×24½" rectangle

Assemble the Border

1. Referring to Assemble the Star Blocks, Step 3, on *page 104*, use the gold print C pieces and the solid dark green C pieces to make a total of 12 pieced star center units. Each unit should measure 2½" square, including the seam allowances.

2. Referring to the photograph *above* for placement, lay out and join the pieced star center units in a single row to make a pieced patchwork strip. Press the seam allowances in one direction. The pieced patchwork strip should measure 2½×24½", including the seam allowances.

3. Sew a yellow stripe 1×24½" strip to the top and bottom edges of the patchwork strip to complete the border strip. Press the seam allowances toward yellow stripe strips. The border strip should measure 3½×24½", including the seam allowances.

Complete the Travel Bag

1. Sew a dark green stripe 4½×24½" rectangle to the bottom edge of the border strip and a dark green stripe 11×24½" rectangle to the top edge. Press all seam allowances toward the dark green stripe rectangles.

2. With the right side inside, fold the pieced rectangle in half crosswise to make a 12½×18" rectangle. Sew across the bottom of the rectangle and up the side edge, stopping 1½" from the top edge. Clip the seam allowance where the stitching stops. Press the seam allowance open above the clip mark.

3. Turn the raw edge of the bag under ¼" and press. Then turn under another ½" to create a casing. Edgestitch the casing in place, stitching close to the folded edge.

4. Insert the cording through the casing for a drawstring. Knot the ends together.

A love of historical indigo print fabrics inspired designer Cindy Blackberg to create a quilt where they could star. Called DaGama indigos, these prints were first produced in Central Europe. In the 1850s, German immigrants introduced them to South Africa, where today they're printed exclusively.

STAR *Chain*

Materials

7 yards of cream print for blocks, setting squares
   and rectangles, and binding

20—18" squares of assorted indigo prints for blocks

5⅞ yards of backing fabric

74×104" of quilt batting

Finished quilt top: 67½×97½"
Finished block: 5" square

Quantities specified for 44/45"-wide, 100% cotton fabrics. All measurements include a ¼" seam allowance. Sew with right sides together unless otherwise stated.

Cut the Fabrics

To make the best use of your fabrics, cut the pieces in the order that follows. There are no pattern pieces for this project; the letter designations are for placement only.

From cream print, cut:
- 9—2½×42" binding strips
- 7—15½" squares for setting
- 10—15½×10½" rectangles for setting
- 58—5½" squares for position E
- 264—1¾" squares for position D
- 264—1¾×3" rectangles for position A
- 130—2⅛" squares, cutting each in half diagonally for a total of 260 triangles for position F

continued

indigo print B squares. (To prevent your fabric from stretching as you draw the lines, place 220-grit sandpaper under the squares.)

3. Align a marked indigo print B square with one end of a cream print A rectangle (see Diagram 1; note the placement of the marked line). Stitch on the marked line; trim the seam allowance to ¼". Press the attached triangle open.

4. Align a second marked indigo print B square with the opposite end of the cream print A rectangle (see Diagram 1, again noting the placement of the marked line). Stitch on the marked line; trim and press as before to make a Flying Geese unit. The pieced Flying Geese unit should still measure 1¾×3", including the seam allowances.

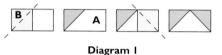

Diagram 1

5. Repeat steps 3 and 4 to make a total of four Flying Geese units.

6. Referring to Diagram 2 for placement, lay out the four Flying Geese units and the remaining squares in three horizontal rows. Sew together the pieces in each row. Press the seam allowances toward the squares. Then join the rows to make a star block. Press the seam allowances in one direction. The pieced star block should measure 5½" square, including the seam allowances.

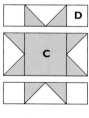

Diagram 2

7. Repeat steps 1 through 6 to make a total of 66 star blocks.

Assemble the Units
Unit 1

1. Referring to Diagram 3, lay out five star blocks and four cream print E squares in three horizontal rows. Sew together the squares in each row. Press the seam allowances toward the cream print E

Star Attractions

From assorted indigo prints, cut:
- 66—3" squares for position C
- 528—1¾" squares for position B (Quiltmaker Cindy Blackberg cut 66 sets of 8 squares from the same fabric.)
- 130—2⅛" squares, cutting each in half diagonally for a total of 260 triangles for position F

Assemble the Star Blocks

1. For one star block you'll need four cream print D squares, four cream print A rectangles, and one set of matching indigo print pieces (one C square and eight B squares).

2. For accurate sewing lines, use a quilter's pencil to mark a diagonal line on the wrong side of the

squares. Then join the rows to make a Unit 1. Press the seam allowances in one direction. Pieced Unit 1 should measure 15½" square, including the seam allowances.

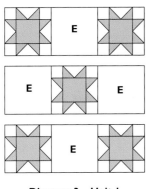

Diagram 3 – Unit 1

2. Repeat steps 1 and 2 to make a total of eight of Unit 1.

Unit 2

1. Referring to Diagram 4, lay out three star blocks and three cream print E squares in two horizontal rows. Sew together the squares in each row. Press the seam allowances toward the cream print E squares. Then join the rows to make a Unit 2. Press the seam allowance in one direction. Pieced Unit 2 should measure 15½×10½", including the seam allowances.

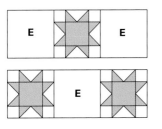

Diagram 4 – Unit 2

2. Repeat steps 1 and 2 to make a total of six of Unit 2.

Unit 3

1. Referring to Diagram 5, lay out two star blocks and two cream print E squares in two horizontal rows. Sew together the squares in each row. Press the seam allowances toward the cream print E squares. Then join the rows to make a Unit 3. Press the seam allowance in one direction. Pieced Unit 3 should measure 10½" square, including the seam allowances.

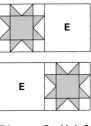

Diagram 5 – Unit 3

2. Repeat Step 1 to make a total of four of Unit 3.

Assemble the Quilt Center

1. Referring to the photograph *opposite* for placement, lay out the 18 pieced units, the seven cream print 15½" setting squares, and the 10 cream print 15½×10½" setting rectangles in seven horizontal rows. Sew together the pieces in each row. Press the seam allowances toward the cream print setting squares or rectangles.

2. Then join the rows to complete the quilt center. Press the seam allowances in one direction. The pieced quilt center should measure 65½×95½", including the seam allowances.

Assemble and Add the Border

1. Sew together one indigo print F triangle and one cream print F triangle to make a triangle-square (see Diagram 6). Press the seam allowance toward the indigo print triangle. The pieced triangle-square should measure 1¾" square, including the seam allowances. Repeat to make a total of 260 triangle-squares.

Diagram 6

2. Referring to the photograph *opposite,* lay out 76 triangle-squares in a vertical row. Sew together the triangle-squares to make a side border strip. Press the seam allowances in one direction. The side border strip should measure 1¾×95½", including the seam allowances. Repeat to make a second side border strip. Join the side border strips to the side edges of the pieced quilt center.

3. Lay out 54 triangle-squares in a horizontal row. Sew together the triangle-squares to make the top border strip. Press the seam allowances in one direction. The top border strip should measure

continued

1¾×68", including the seam allowances. Repeat to make a matching bottom border strip. Join the border strips to the top and bottom edges of the pieced quilt center to complete the quilt top.

Complete the Quilt

1. Layer the quilt top, batting, and backing according to the instructions in Quilter's Schoolhouse, which begins on *page 145*.

2. Quilt as desired. The photographed quilt was hand-quilted with an X in the stars and a feathered square design in the large blocks. A smaller feathered square design was quilted in the small blocks, and a line was quilted in the border ¼" from the triangle points.

3. Use the cream print 2½×42" strips to bind the quilt according to the instructions in Quilter's Schoolhouse.

Star Chain Quilt
optional sizes

If you'd like to make this quilt in a size other than for a twin bed, use the information *below*.

Alternate quilt sizes	Wall	Full/Queen
Number of blocks	45	97
Number of Unit 1	5	13
Finished size	67½" square	97½" square
Yardage requirements		
Cream print	4⅝ yards	9¼ yards
Assorted indigo prints	1¾ yards total	3 yards total
Backing	4⅛ yards	8⅔ yards
Batting	74" square	104" square

MINI QUILT

Whether it's a wall hanging or a tablecloth for a doll's tea party, the "Star Chain" mini quilt takes on a new look in shades of rose.

Materials

⅛ yard of cream print for blocks and inner border

7×15" rectangle of tan print for blocks

½ yard of rose print for blocks, outer border, and binding

7×7" square of pink print for blocks

⅛ yard of brown print for block borders

¼ yard of rose tone-on-tone print for sashing

⅞ yard of backing fabric

29" square of quilt batting

Finished quilt top: 22½" square
Finished block: 5" square

Cut the Fabrics

To make the best use of your fabrics, cut the pieces in the order that follows. The border strip measurements are mathematically correct. You may wish to cut your border strips longer than specified to allow for possible sewing differences. There are no pattern pieces for this project; the letter designations are for placement only.

From cream print, cut:
• 16—1¾" squares for position D
• 2—1×18" inner border strips
• 2—1×17" inner border strips
From tan print, cut:
• 16—1¾×3" rectangles for position A
From rose print, cut:
• 2—3×23" outer border strips
• 2—3×18" outer border strips
• 3—2×42" binding strips
• 32—1¾" squares for position B
From pink print, cut:
• 4—3" squares for position C
From brown print, cut:
• 8—1×6½" border strips
• 8—1×5½" border strips

From rose tone-on-tone print, cut:
- 2—2×17" sashing strips
- 3—2×14" sashing strips
- 2—2×6½" sashing strips

Assemble the Star Blocks

1. Referring to the Assemble the Star Blocks instructions on *page 112*, use four cream print D squares, four tan print A rectangles, eight rose print B squares, and one pink print C square to make a star block.

2. Sew a brown print 1×5½" border strip to the top and bottom edges of the star block. Then add a brown print 1×6½" border strip to each side edge of the star block to make a bordered star block. Press the seam allowances toward the brown print border. The bordered star block should measure 6½" square, including the seam allowances.

3. Repeat steps 1 and 2 to make a total of four bordered star blocks.

Add the Sashing

1. Referring to the photograph *below*, lay out the four bordered star blocks and the two rose tone-on-tone print 2×6½" sashing strips in two vertical rows. Sew together the pieces in each row. Press the seam allowances toward the sashing. Join the rows with a rose tone-on-tone print 2×14" sashing strip to make the quilt center. Press the seam allowances in one direction. The pieced quilt center should measure 14" square.

2. Sew a rose tone-on-tone print 2×14" sashing strip to each side edge of the pieced quilt center. Then

add a rose tone-on-tone print 2×17" sashing strip to the top and bottom edges of the pieced quilt center. Press the seam allowances toward the rose tone-on-tone print sashing strips. The pieced quilt center should now measure 17" square, including the seam allowances.

Add the Borders

1. Sew a cream print 1×17" inner border strip to opposite edges of the pieced quilt center. Then add a cream print 1×18" inner border strip to the remaining raw edges of the pieced quilt center. Press all seam allowances toward the cream print inner border.

2. Sew a rose print 3×18" outer border strip to opposite edges of the pieced quilt center. Then add a rose print 3×23" outer border strip to the remaining raw edges of the pieced quilt center to complete the quilt top. Press all seam allowances toward the rose print border.

Complete the Quilt

1. Layer the quilt top, batting, and backing according to the instructions in Quilter's Schoolhouse, which begins on *page 145*. Quilt as desired.

2. Use the rose print 2×42" strips to bind the quilt according to the instructions in Quilter's Schoolhouse.

SHEET SET

If you're making the "Star Chain" quilt for your bed, why not make a coordinating sheet set as well? You could use extra blocks made from the same fabrics as the quilt, or choose related fabrics, as we did.

Materials

¾ yard total of assorted white prints for blocks

¾ yard total of assorted light blue prints for blocks

⅝ yard of white tone-on-tone print for
    cording cover

5¾ yards of ¼"-diameter cotton cording

Purchased full-size flat bedsheet

Finished star border: 5×94½"
Finished block: 5" square

(*Note:* This border strip was made for a full-size sheet. Make more or fewer blocks depending upon the width of your sheet.)

Cut the Fabrics

To make the best use of your fabrics, cut the pieces in the order that follows. There are no pattern pieces for this project; the letter designations are for placement only.

From assorted white prints, cut:
- 152—1¾" squares for position B
- 19—3" squares for position C

From assorted light blue prints, cut:
- 76—1¾" squares for position D
- 76—1¾×3" rectangles for position A

From white tone-on-tone print, cut:
- 1—20" square, cutting it into enough 1½"-wide bias strips to total 198" in length for covered cording (For specific instructions on cutting bias strips, see Quilter's Schoolhouse, which begins on *page 145*.)

Assemble the Star Blocks

Referring to the Assemble the Star Blocks instructions on *page 112*, use eight white print B squares, one white print C square, four light blue print D squares, and four light blue A rectangles to make a star block. Repeat to make a total of 19 star blocks.

Assemble the Star Border

1. Referring to the photograph *opposite* for placement, lay out the blocks in a row. Sew together the blocks to make a star block border. Press the seam allowances in one direction. The pieced star block border should measure 5½×95½", including the seam allowances.

2. Using the white tone-on-tone print 1½"-wide bias strips and the ¼"-diameter cording, create 198" of covered cording (see Quilter's Schoolhouse for specific instructions). Cut the covered cording into two 99"-long pieces.

3. Aligning the raw edges, sew a length of covered cording to one edge of the star block border. Join the remaining covered cording piece to the opposite edge of the star border. Turn the raw edges under and press.

Complete the Sheet

1. Pin the star block border over the bedsheet's top band with right sides up; abut one edge of the border with the lower edge of the band. Trim the short edges of the star block border ½" beyond the side edges of the sheet. Turn under a ½" hem on each short edge.

2. Stitch in the ditch along both long edges of the border between the cording and the star blocks and ¼" from the folded short edges to attach the border to the sheet.

PILLOWCASES

A coordinating band accents the edge.

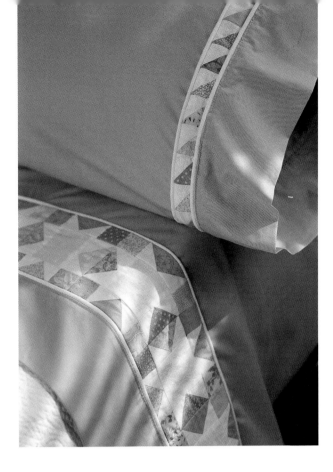

Materials for two pillowcases

¼ yard total of assorted white prints for triangle-squares

¼ yard total of assorted light blue prints for triangle-squares

½ yard of white tone-on-tone print for cording cover

5 yards of ¼"-diameter cotton cording

Two purchased standard-size pillowcases

Finished triangle-square border: 1¼×40"

(*Note:* This border strip was made for a standard-size pillowcase. Make more or fewer triangle-squares depending upon the width of your pillowcase.)

Cut the Fabrics

To make the best use of your fabrics, cut the pieces in the order that follows.

From assorted white prints, cut:
• 32—2⅛" squares, cutting each in half diagonally for a total of 64 triangles

From assorted light blue prints, cut:
• 32—2⅛" squares, cutting each in half diagonally for a total of 64 triangles

From white tone-on-tone print, cut:
• 1—18" square, cutting them into enough 1½"-wide bias strips to total 180" in length for covered cording (For specific instructions on cutting bias strips, see Quilter's Schoolhouse, which begins on *page 145.*)

Assemble the Triangle-Squares

Referring to the Assemble and Add the Border instructions, Step 1, on *page 113,* use the white print and blue print triangles to make a total of 64 triangle-squares.

Assemble the Border

1. Lay out 32 triangle-squares in a row. Sew together the squares to make a border strip. Press the seam allowances in one direction. The pieced border strip should measure 1¾×40½", including the seam allowances. Repeat to make a second pieced border strip.

2. Using the white tone-on-tone print 1½"-wide bias strips and the ¼"-diameter cording, create 180" of covered cording (see Quilter's Schoolhouse for instructions). Cut the covered cording into four 45"-long pieces.

3. Aligning raw edges, sew a length of covered cording to each long edge of the pieced border. With the right sides inside, sew together the short edges of the border strips; turn the strips right sides out.

Complete the Pillowcases

Pin a border strip over a pillowcase band with both right sides up; abut one edge of the border with the lower edge of the pillowcase band. Stitch in the ditch along both sides of the border between the cording and the triangle-squares. Sew the remaining border strip to the second pillowcase in the same manner.

ALL ABOUT APPLIQUÉ

No longer the tedious handwork of yesteryear, appliqué has been transformed by today's timesaving tools and techniques. Here you can choose from fusible folk art motifs, blanket-stitched wool projects, and hand- or machine-sewn traditional patterns. Experimenting with these projects will allow you to quickly expand your appliqué repertoire.

SOWN
Fabric

Rather than garden with flowers

or vegetables, designer Marty Freed

cultivates carefully selected fabrics

into quilts. Newer fabrics are "sown"

in like the latest hybrids, while

personal favorites appear year after

year like old-fashioned perennials.

For this project, Marty picked

a scrappy assortment of prints

and planted them alongside stripes

and checks in light, medium,

and dark tones.

Materials

2 yards of beige print for center medallion, house
blocks, and Nine-Patch blocks

1 yard total of assorted print scraps in red, rust,
brown, blue, gold, green, and white for appliqués

½ yard of dark blue print for medallion border

½ yard of off-white print for medallion border

½ yard of cream print for medallion border corners

¼ yard *each* of 30 assorted prints for
Nine-Patch blocks

¼ yard *each* of eight assorted light, medium, and
dark prints for house blocks

¼ yard *each* of seven assorted medium and
dark prints for plain blocks

2¼ yards of medium-dark print for outer border
and binding

5 yards of backing fabric

79×90" of quilt batting

2 yards of fusing-adhesive material

2 yards of tear-away stabilizer

Gold thread for machine appliqué

continued

Quilt Assembly Diagram

Finished quilt top: 72½×83½"
Finished block: 5½" square

Quantities specified for 44/45"-wide, 100% cotton fabrics. All measurements include a ¼" seam allowance. Sew with right sides together unless otherwise stated.

Cut the Fabrics

For this project, the cutting and assembly instructions have been divided into sections (designated by the heavy black lines in the Quilt Assembly Diagram). To make the best use of your fabrics, cut the pieces in the order listed in each section. The patterns are on *Pattern Sheet 1*. To use fusing-adhesive material for appliqué, as was done in this project, complete the following steps.

I. Lay the fusing-adhesive material, paper side up, over the patterns. With a pencil, trace each piece the specified number of times, leaving ½" between tracings. Cut out the pieces roughly ¼" outside of the traced lines.

2. Following the manufacturer's instructions, press the fusing-adhesive material shapes onto the backs of the designated fabrics; let cool. Cut out the shapes on the drawn lines. Peel off the paper backings.

Appliqué the Center Medallion

From beige print, cut:
• 1—32½" foundation square

From assorted red print scraps, cut:
• 1 *each* of patterns A and B
• 4 *each* of patterns L and T
• 2 of Pattern R

From assorted rust print scraps, cut:
• 2 *each* of patterns E, F, and K
• 4 of Pattern G
• 1 of Pattern S

From assorted brown print scraps, cut:
• 1 of Pattern D
• 2 *each* of patterns H, O, and P
• 3 of Pattern S

From assorted blue print scraps, cut:
• 1 *each* of patterns A, B, and I
• 2 of patterns C, O, P, and R
• 4 *each* of Pattern S reversed

From assorted gold print scraps, cut:
• 1 *each* of patterns D and I
• 4 of Pattern Q

From assorted green print scraps, cut:
• 2 of Pattern J
• 4 *each* of patterns M and U
• 8 of Pattern N
• 12 of Pattern V

From white print scraps, cut:
• 2 of Pattern W

From dark blue print, cut:
• 16 of Pattern X

From off-white print, cut:
• 12 of Pattern X

From cream print, cut:
• 4 of Pattern Y

I. Fold the beige print 32½" square appliqué foundation in half horizontally, vertically, and diagonally; finger-press to create positioning guides for the appliqué pieces.

2. Referring to Diagram 1, position the appliqué pieces on the foundation square, overlapping where necessary. When the appliqué pieces are correctly positioned, fuse them in place with a hot, dry iron; let the fabrics cool.

Diagram 1

3. Position the tear-away stabilizer under the foundation square. Using the gold thread and a buttonhole stitch, machine-appliqué the pieces to the foundation square to create the center medallion.

4. After you've completed the stitching, tear away the stabilizer; use tweezers to get into small places. Press the center medallion and trim it to 31¼" square, including the seam allowances.

5. Referring to Diagram 2 for placement, sew together four dark blue print and three off-white print X triangles, alternating dark and light, to make a medallion border strip. Repeat to make a total of four medallion border strips.

Diagram 2

6. Sew one medallion border strip to each edge of the center medallion. Press the seam allowances toward the border. Sew a cream print Y triangle to each corner.

7. Position the remaining appliqué pieces on the corner triangles. Referring to Step 3, stabilize the corner triangles, and machine-appliqué the pieces in place to complete the quilt center. The pieced quilt center should measure 39" square, including the seam allowances.

Piece the Border Blocks
For Nine-Patch Blocks
From beige print, cut:
- 120—1⅞×3¼" rectangles

From *each* of 30 assorted prints, cut:
- 4—1⅞" squares
- 1—3¼" square

1. Referring to Diagram 3, lay out four 1⅞" squares and one 3¼" square in the same print and four beige print 1⅞×3¼" rectangles. Sew together the pieces in rows. Press the seam allowances toward the darker pieces. Then join the rows to make a Nine-Patch block. Press the seam allowances in one direction. The pieced block should measure 6" square, including the seam allowances.

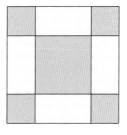

Diagram 3

2. Repeat Step 1 to make a total of 30 Nine-Patch blocks.

For House Block No. 1
From beige print, cut:
- 8—1¼×6" rectangles for position 1A
- 4—2⅞" squares, cutting them in half diagonally for a total of 8 triangles for position 1B

From *each* of four light prints, cut:
- 3—1¼×1½" rectangles for position 1H
- 1—1¼×2" rectangle for position 1G

continued

2. Sew together the pieces in the sections designated in the diagram. Then join the sections to make a house block No. 1. The pieced block should measure 6" square, including the seam allowances.

3. Repeat steps 1 and 2 to make a total of four of house block No. 1.

For House Block No. 2
From beige print, cut:
• 4—1×6" rectangles for position 2A
• 4 *each* of patterns 2B and 2B reversed
From *each of four light prints, cut:*
• 1—1½×2¼" rectangle for position 2H
• 2—1¼×2¼" rectangles for position 2G
• 1 of Pattern 2I
From *each of four medium prints, cut:*
• 3—1×4" rectangles for position 2C
• 2—1¼×1¾" rectangles for position 2D
• 2—1¼×1" rectangles for position 2E
• 1 of Pattern 2J
From *each of four dark prints, cut:*
• 2—1×4" rectangles for position 2C
• 1—1½×2¼" rectangle for position 2F

I. Referring to Diagram 5, lay out the pieces for one house block No. 2.

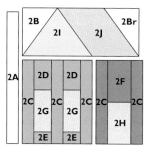

Diagram 5

2. Sew together the pieces in the sections designated in the diagram. Then join the sections to make a house block No. 2. The pieced block should measure 6" square, including seam allowances.

3. Repeat steps 1 and 2 to make a total of four of house block No. 2.

From *each* of four medium prints, cut:
• 1—3¾" square, cutting it in half diagonally to make a total of 2 triangles for position 1C (there will be 1 of *each* left over)
From *each* of four dark prints, cut:
• 2—1¼×4" rectangles for position 1D
• 1—1½×4" rectangle for position 1E
• 5—1¼×1" rectangles for position 1F

I. Referring to Diagram 4, lay out the pieces for one house block No. 1.

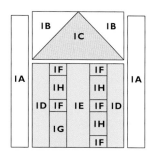

Diagram 4

For House Block No. 3

From beige print, cut:
- 4—3⅝" squares, cutting them in half diagonally for a total of 8 triangles for position 3A

From *each* of four light prints, cut:
- 4—1×2" rectangles for position 3H
- 1—1½×2½" rectangle for position 3I

From *each* of four medium prints, cut:
- 2—¾×3¼" rectangles for position 3C
- 4—1×3¼" rectangles for position 3D
- 4—1×1¼" rectangles for position 3E
- 1—1½×1¼" rectangle for position 3F
- 4—1" squares for position 3G

From *each* of four dark prints, cut:
- 1—4¾" square, cutting it in half diagonally for a total of 2 triangles for position 3B (you'll have 1 of *each* left over)

1. Referring to Diagram 6, lay out the pieces for one house block No. 3.

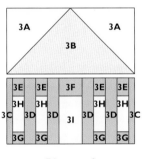

Diagram 6

2. Sew together the pieces in the sections designated in the diagram. Then join the sections to make a house block No. 3. The pieced block should measure 6" square, including the seam allowances.

3. Repeat steps 1 and 2 to make a total of four of house block No. 3.

For House Block No. 4

From beige print, cut:
- 4 *each* of patterns 4A and 4A reversed
- 8—1×3¾" rectangles for position 4B

From *each* of four light prints, cut:
- 1—2¼×2" rectangle for position 4H
- 1—1½×2¼" rectangle for position 4I

From *each* of four medium prints, cut:
- 2—1×3¾" rectangles for position 4B
- 1—1½×2" rectangle for position 4D

- 1—1¼×3¾" rectangle for position 4E
- 1—2¼×1¾" rectangle for position 4F
- 1—2¼×1" rectangle for position 4G

From *each* of four dark prints, cut:
- 1 of Pattern 4C

1. Referring to Diagram 7, lay out the pieces for one house block No. 4.

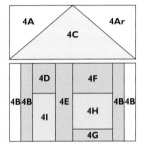

Diagram 7

2. Sew together the pieces in the sections designated in the diagram. Then join the sections to make a house block No. 4. The pieced block should measure 6" square, including the seam allowances.

3. Repeat steps 1 and 2 to make a total of four of house block No. 4.

Add the Pieced Border

From *each* of seven assorted medium and dark prints, cut:
- 7—6" squares

1. Referring to the Quilt Assembly Diagram on *page 122*, lay out the quilt center, 48 medium and dark print 6" squares (you'll have 1 left over), the 16 house blocks, and the 30 Nine-Patch blocks.

2. Sew together the border pieces in the sections as designated in the diagram. Press the seam allowances in one direction, alternating the direction with each row.

3. Join the short border sections to opposite edges of the pieced quilt center. Then join the long border sections to the remaining edges of the pieced quilt center. Press the seam allowances toward the border. The pieced quilt center should now measure 61×72", including the seam allowances.

Sown Fabric

continued

Add the Outer Border

Cut the outer border and binding strips lengthwise (parallel to the selvage). Before cutting the border strips, measure your pieced quilt center to check for possible sewing differences.

From medium-dark print, cut:
- 2—6½×73" outer border strips
- 2—6½×72" outer border strips
- 4—2½×80" binding strips

Sew a short outer border strip to each side edge of the pieced quilt center. Then add a long outer border strip to the top and bottom edges of the pieced quilt center to complete the quilt top. Press the seam allowances toward the outer border.

Complete the Quilt

1. Layer the quilt top, batting, and backing according to the instructions in Quilter's Schoolhouse, which begins on *page 145*.

2. Quilt as desired. Quiltmaker Marty Freed used ecru perle cotton thread to hand-quilt this project with long stitches (sometimes referred to as utility stitches).

3. Use the medium-dark print 2½×80" strips to bind the quilt according to the instructions in Quilter's Schoolhouse.

ROW QUILT

Repeat the Nine-Patch block and two house blocks from "Sown Fabric" to make this simple row quilt.

Materials

½ yard of cream print for blocks and inner border

¼ yard of black print for blocks

⅓ yard of red print No. 1 for blocks and sashing

⅛ yard of red print No. 2 for blocks

¼ yard of muslin for blocks

⅛ yard of yellow print for blocks

⅔ yard of black polka dot for blocks, outer border, and binding

⅞ yard of backing fabric

30×42" of quilt batting

All About Appliqué

Finished quilt top: 23½×36½"
Finished block: 5½" square

Cut the Fabrics

To make the best use of your fabrics, cut the pieces in the order that follows. This project uses patterns 4A and 4C from the "Sown Fabric" project, which are on *Pattern Sheet 1*. The other numbers and letters are placement designations.

From cream print, cut:
- 6—3¼" squares
- 24—1⅞" squares
- 2—1½×33" inner border strips
- 2—1½×18" inner border strips
- 3—1¼×2" rectangles for position 1G
- 3—1½×2¼" rectangles for position 4I

From black print, cut:
- 24—1⅞×3¼" rectangles
- 2—3¾" squares, cutting them in half diagonally for a total of 4 triangles for position 1C (there will be 1 left over)

From red print No. 1, cut:
- 2—1×31" sashing strips
- 6—1×17" sashing strips
- 6—1×3¾" rectangles for position 4B
- 3—1½×2" rectangles for position 4D
- 3—1¼×3¾" rectangles for position 4E
- 3—2¼×1¾" rectangles for position 4F
- 3—2¼×1" rectangles for position 4G

From red print No. 2, cut:
- 6—1¼×4" rectangles for position 1D
- 3—1½×4" rectangles for position 1E
- 15—1¼×1" rectangles for position 1F

From muslin, cut:
- 6—1¼×6" rectangles for position 1A
- 3—2⅞" squares, cutting them in half diagonally for a total of 6 triangles for position 1B
- 3 *each* of patterns 4A and 4A reversed
- 6—1×3¾" rectangles for position 4B

From yellow print, cut:
- 12—1⅞×3¼" rectangles
- 9—1¼×1½" rectangles for position 1H
- 3—2¼×2" rectangles for position 4H

From black polka dot, cut:
- 3—2½×42" binding strips
- 2—2½×37" outer border strips
- 2—2½×20" outer border strips
- 3—3¼" squares
- 12—1⅞" squares
- 3 of Pattern 4C

Assemble the Blocks

1. Referring to the Piece the Border Blocks instructions on *page 123*, make a Nine-Patch block using four cream print 1⅞" squares, four black print 1⅞×3¼" rectangles, and one cream print 3¼" square. Repeat to make a total of six black-and-cream Nine-Patch blocks.

2. Make a Nine-Patch block using four black polka dot 1⅞" squares, four yellow print 1⅞×3¼" rectangles, and one black polka dot 3¼" square. Repeat to make a total of three yellow-and-black Nine-Patch blocks.

3. Referring to the Piece the Border Blocks instructions on *page 123*, make a house block No. 1 using the position 1A to 1H pieces. Repeat to make a total of three of house block No. 1.

4. Referring to the Piece the Border Blocks instructions on *page 125*, make a house block No. 4 using the position 4A to 4I pieces. Repeat to make a total of three of house block No. 4.

continued

Assemble the Quilt Top

1. Sew together three black-and-cream Nine-Patch blocks in a horizontal row. Press the seam allowances toward the center block. The pieced row should measure 6×17", including the seam allowances. Repeat to make a second row of black-and-cream Nine-Patch blocks. Then repeat to make a row of yellow-and-black Nine-Patch blocks.

2. In the same manner, sew together a row of the three house block No. 1s, pressing the seam allowances away from the center block. The pieced row should measure 6×17", including the seam allowances. Repeat to make a row of the three house block No. 4s.

3. Referring to the photograph on *page 126*, lay out the three Nine-Patch rows, the two house block rows, and the six red print 1×17" sashing strips. Join the rows, pressing the seam allowances in one direction. Then join the red print 1×31" sashing strips to each side edge to complete the pieced quilt center. The pieced quilt center should measure 18×31", including the seam allowances.

4. Sew a cream print 1½×18" inner border strip to the top and bottom edges of the pieced quilt center. Then join a cream print 1½×33" inner border strip to each side edge of the pieced quilt center. Press the seam allowances toward the inner border. The pieced quilt center should now measure 20×33", including the seam allowances.

5. Sew a black polka dot 2½×20" outer border strip to the top and bottom edges of the pieced quilt center. Then join a black polka dot 2½×37" outer border strip to each side edge of the pieced quilt center to complete the quilt top. Press the seam allowances toward the outer border.

Complete the Quilt

1. Layer the quilt top, batting, and backing according to the directions in Quilter's Schoolhouse, which begins on *page 145*.

2. Quilt as desired. The blocks in this quilt were machine-quilted in the ditch.

3. Use the black polka dot 2½×42" strips to bind the quilt according to the directions in Quilter's Schoolhouse.

APPLIQUÉ DRESS AND JACKET

Select your favorite appliqués from

the "Sown Fabric" quilt to add flair to

a basic dress and jacket ensemble.

Materials

Scraps of red, orange, yellow, green, teal, blue, and

   violet prints for appliqués

Purchased black linen dress and jacket

1/2 yard of fusing-adhesive material

1/2 yard of tear-away stabilizer

Matching or contrasting threads for

   machine appliqué

Cut the Fabrics

To make the best use of your fabrics, cut the pieces
in the order that follows. This project uses "Sown
Fabric" patterns, which are on *Pattern Sheet 1.*
For this project we used fusing-adhesive material
for appliquéing. To use this same method, follow
the Cut the Fabrics instructions, steps 1 and 2, on
page 122.

From red print, cut:
• 1 *each* of patterns A, F, and P
From orange print, cut:
• 2 of Pattern Q
From yellow print, cut:
• 1 *each* of patterns B, E, and W
• 2 of Pattern O
• 1 of Pattern D (optional)
From green print, cut:
• 1 of Pattern C
• 2 of Pattern M
• 4 of Pattern N
From teal print, cut:
• 1 *each* of patterns K and P
From blue print, cut:
• 1 *each* of patterns F and P
From violet print, cut:
• 2 of Pattern L
• 1 *each* of patterns E and O
• 1 of Pattern D (optional)

Assemble the Appliqué

1. Referring to the photographs *opposite and above,*
   position the appliqués on the dress front and
   jacket as desired. *Note:* On the featured garment, a
   tapered satin stitch was used for the butterfly

bodies; optional Pattern D may be used instead
of the stitching. Fuse the appliqués in place
following the manufacturer's instructions. Let the
fabrics cool.

2. Position tear-away stabilizer under the garment
   areas being appliquéd; satin-stitch the appliqué
   pieces in place using matching or contrasting
   thread. Begin with the bottom layer of each
   appliqué and work toward the top layer.

3. Satin-stitch a pair of 1- to 1½"-long antennae
   extending from the top of each butterfly body.

I Love *You*

Janet Carija Brandt's interpretation of a traditional folk art pattern

will add a new dimension to your stitching repertoire. She combines aspects

of embroidery, appliqué, and quilting for this heartwarming

wool-on-wool penny rug.

Materials

½ yard of solid cream wool for appliqué foundation

    and appliqués

11½×14½" rectangle of pink print cotton

    for backing

10×13" of thin quilt batting

Embroidery floss: pink and ivory

Finished penny rug top: 12½×15½"

Designer Notes

Designer Janet Carija Brandt always prewashes wool fabric before using it in a project. This process felts the wool, which results in crisp, clean-cut edges that don't need to be turned under and will not ravel.

To felt wool, machine-wash it in a hot-water wash/cool rinse cycle with a small amount of detergent, machine-dry, and steam-press.

Cut the Fabrics

To make the best use of your fabrics, cut the pieces in the order that follows. The patterns are on *Pattern Sheet 1*. To make templates of the patterns, follow the instructions in Quilter's Schoolhouse, which begins on *page 145*.

Remember: Do not add any seam allowances when cutting out the appliqué shapes from felted wool.

From solid cream wool, cut:
- 1—10½×13½" rectangle for appliqué foundation
- 2—⅜×10½" bias strips (See Cut Bias Strips in Quilter's Schoolhouse, for specific instructions.)
- 2—⅜×5" bias strips

continued

- 1 *each* of patterns A, F, H, I reversed, K, L, M, N, O, P, Q, R, S, T, U, V, W, X, and Y
- 5 of Pattern B
- 2 *each* of patterns C, E, and I
- 6 *each* of patterns G and J
- 3 of Pattern D

Appliqué and Embroider the Center

1. Referring to the photograph on *page 131* for placement, arrange the four bias strips and pieces A through U on the solid cream wool foundation. Once you're pleased with the arrangement, pin the pieces in place.

2. Using two strands of pink embroidery floss, blanket-stitch around each wool shape. Work from the bottom layer to the top. Janet leaves her pieces pinned in place for as long as possible, lifting up only those parts of the appliqué pieces that are in the way of where she's stitching.

   To blanket-stitch, refer to the diagram *below*. Begin by pulling the needle up at A. Form a reverse L shape with the floss, and hold the angle of the L shape in place with your thumb. Push the needle down at B and come up at C to secure the stitch. Repeat until you've stitched around the shape.

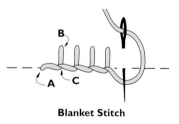

Blanket Stitch

3. Once all of the pieces have been stitched in place, use two strands of pink embroidery floss to add a French knot to each of the appliquéd birds for eyes.

   To make a French knot, refer to the diagram *above right*. Begin by bringing the needle up at A. Wrap the floss around the needle one to three times without twisting the floss. Insert the needle back into the fabric at B, 1/16" away from A. Gently push the floss wraps down the needle to meet the fabric. Pull the floss through the fabric to the back. To vary the size and shape of French knots, wrap the floss around the needle up to six times or make the wraps tighter or looser.

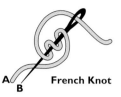

French Knot

4. Using two strands of pink embroidery floss, chain-stitch tail feather and wing lines on each appliquéd bird and a solid heart on each appliquéd heart. For the hearts, Janet suggests working from the outer edge to the center.

   To chain-stitch, refer to the diagram *below*. Begin by bringing the needle up at A. Make a loop. Holding the loop in place, go back down at A and come up at B, about 1/4" from A. Pull floss taut. Continue in the same manner until the desired shape is created.

Chain Stitch

5. Steam-press the appliquéd foundation on the wrong side only.

Complete the Penny Rug

1. Position the straight edge of the solid cream V, W, X, and Y strips 1/4" under the edges of the appliquéd foundation. Using two strands of pink embroidery floss, blanket-stitch the strips to the foundation. Then blanket-stitch around the scalloped edge of each strip to complete the penny rug top.

2. Layer the penny rug top, batting, and backing according to the instructions in Quilter's Schoolhouse, which begins on *page 145*. Janet recommends basting the layers with safety pins.

3. Quilt as desired. Janet hand-quilted her project around the appliqué shapes and 1/16" from the blanket stitching with two strands of ivory embroidery floss.

4. Trim the batting to the exact size of the appliquéd foundation. Trim the backing fabric 1/4" beyond the batting. Fold the backing edges over the batting, hiding the raw edges under the penny rug top. Slip-stitch the backing to the penny rug top to complete the penny rug.

GRANDMOTHER'S HANDPRINT QUILT

Using handprints in the center square to represent her children and ringing the outer edge with a handprint for every grandchild, this quilt was designed as a tribute to a special grandmother. Modify the design to reflect the members of your mother's or grandmother's family.

Materials

24×28" rectangle of bright green felted wool for appliqué foundation

22—5" squares of felted wool in assorted purple, blue, and raspberry for appliqués

2—5" squares of yellow felted wool for appliqués

1—5" square of pink felted wool for appliqués

⅛ yard of dark blue felted wool for inner border

¼ yard of dark purple felted wool for outer border

24×28" rectangle of purple print cotton for backing

Perle cotton thread in matching colors, plus assorted greens

Cut the Fabrics

This project uses felted wool. To felt wool, see Designer Notes on *page 130* for instructions.

To make the best use of your fabrics, cut the pieces in the order that follows. This project uses "I Love You" patterns, which are on *Pattern Sheet 1*. To make templates of the patterns, follow the instructions in Quilter's Schoolhouse, which begins on *page 145*. Remember: Do not add any seam allowances when cutting out appliqué shapes from felted wool.

From assorted purple and blue wool, cut:
• 8 of Pattern A
• 9 of Pattern A reversed
• 5 of Pattern F
• 1 of Pattern E

continued

From assorted raspberry wool, cut:
- 3 of Pattern A
- 2 of Pattern A reversed
- 5 of Pattern J
- 1 of Pattern C

From yellow wool, cut:
- 1 of Pattern A
- 5 of Pattern D

From pink wool, cut:
- 4 of Pattern B

From dark blue wool, cut:
- 2—½×16" border strips
- 2—½×15" border strips

From dark purple wool, cut:
- 2—1¼×28" binding strips
- 2—1¼×24" binding strips

Appliqué and Embroider the Foundation

1. Referring to the photograph on *page 133* for placement, in the center of the bright green 24×28" appliqué foundation position the dark blue ½×16" border strips on each side and the dark blue ½×15" border strips on the top and bottom edges to make a rectangle; pin in place. Then position the appliqué pieces as desired. Once you're pleased with the arrangement, pin the pieces in place.

2. Use one strand of matching perle cotton to stitch the inner border and appliqué pieces in place with a blanket stitch, running stitch, or other embroidery stitch (see the Running Stitch diagram *below;* diagrams for other stitches are on *page 132*).

Running Stitch

3. Use one strand of green perle cotton and a chain stitch (see the diagram on *page 132*) or other decorative embroidery stitch to add stems to each flower and handprint inside the inner border to complete the appliqué.

4. Steam press the appliquéd foundation on the wrong side only to prevent flattening the appliqués and stitching.

Complete the Quilt

1. With wrong sides together, layer the appliquéd foundation and the purple print cotton 24×28" rectangle. Pin or baste the layers together. Quilt as desired through all layers.

2. Use the dark purple 1¼×28" strips to bind each side edge of the quilt by wrapping each strip over an edge and sewing through all layers with a running stitch and one strand of matching perle cotton. Repeat with the dark purple 1¼×24" binding strips and the top and bottom edges of the quilt.

GIFT BAG & TAG

Fusible appliqué provides a quick and easy way to make a personalized presentation.

Materials

3×8" rectangle of bright pink print for appliqués

3×8" rectangle of purple print for appliqués

Scrap of bright green print for appliqués

7" square of bright green stripe for appliqués

8×11" rectangle of solid magenta for appliqué foundation

½ yard of fusing-adhesive material

Spray adhesive

⅔ yard of ⅛"-wide teal satin ribbon

7¾×9½×4¾" paper gift bag

3½×7" piece of purple card stock

Hole punch

Cut the Fabrics

To make the best use of your fabrics, cut the pieces in the order that follows. This project uses "I Love You" patterns C and E, which are on *Pattern Sheet 1*. To use fusing-adhesive material for appliquéing, as was done in this project, complete the following steps.

1. Lay the fusing-adhesive material, paper side up, over the patterns. Use a pencil to trace each pattern five times, leaving ½" between tracings. Draw four 2½" squares and one 6" square, leaving ½" between tracings. Cut out the pieces roughly ¼" outside of the traced lines.

2. Following the manufacturer's instructions, press the fusing-adhesive material shapes onto the backs of the fabrics designated *below;* let cool. Cut out the shapes on the drawn lines. Peel off the paper backing.

From bright pink print fabric, cut:
- 2—2½" squares
- 2 of Pattern C

From purple print, cut:
- 2—2½" squares
- 3 of Pattern C

From bright green print, cut:
- 5 of Pattern E

From bright green stripe, cut:
- 1—6" square

From solid magenta, cut:
- 1—7" square
- 1—2½" square

Appliqué the Gift Bag and Tag

1. Center the bright green stripe 6" square on top of the magenta 7" square. Following the manufacturer's instructions, fuse in place; let cool.

2. Referring to the photograph *above* for placement, lay out two purple print 2½" squares and two pink print 2½" squares in two rows centered on the bright green stripe square. Arrange flower appliqué shapes on all four squares, positioning pink print flowers on the purple print squares and purple print flowers on the pink print squares. Fuse in place; let cool.

3. Lay the folded gift bag on a flat surface with the bag front right side up. Following the

manufacturer's instructions, apply spray adhesive to the wrong side of the appliquéd magenta square; adhere the appliquéd magenta square to the front of the tote bag to complete the gift bag.

4. Center the remaining flower appliqué shapes on the solid magenta 2½" square. Fuse in place; let cool.

5. Fold the purple card stock in half to make a square. Apply spray adhesive to the wrong side of the appliquéd magenta square and adhere it to the center front of the folded card stock to make the gift tag.

6. Punch a hole in the upper corner of the gift tag near the fold. Slide the ribbon through the hole and tie the ribbon ends in a bow around the handle to complete the gift tag.

BELLA TULIP
Garden

Hobbyist quiltmaker Helen Downing

combined piecing and appliqué to

make this prizewinning pastel beauty

bloom. After a group of Italian women

complimented her appliqué work

saying it was bella, *or beautiful,*

Helen chose the name for her quilt.

The quilt earned second place in the

bed-size competition of the 1997

Homes & Gardens Challenge.

Materials

6½ yards of solid cream for blocks and border

1¼ yards of solid green for blocks and border

1½ yards of green print for blocks, appliqués, and border

1⅛ yards of solid pink for blocks, appliqués, and binding

2¼ yards of pink print for blocks, appliqués, and border

½ yard of solid blue for blocks and appliqués

½ yard of blue print for blocks and appliqués

¼ yard of solid yellow for blocks and appliqués

⅓ yard of yellow print for blocks and appliqués

7¾ yards of backing fabric

93×106" of quilt batting

Finished quilt top: 86¼×99"
Finished block: 9" square

continued

Quantities specified for 44/45"-wide, 100% cotton fabrics. All measurements include a ¼" seam allowance. Sew with right sides together unless otherwise stated.

Cut the Fabrics

To make the best use of your fabrics, cut the pieces in the order that follows. The patterns are on *Pattern Sheet 2*. To make templates of the patterns, follow the instructions in Quilter's Schoolhouse, which begins on *page 145*. Remember to add a ³⁄₁₆" seam allowance when cutting out each appliqué piece.

Cut the border strips the length of the fabric (parallel to the selvage). Extra length has been added to the appliqué border strips to allow for mitering the corners. The outer border strip measurements are mathematically correct. You may wish to cut your outer border strips longer than specified to allow for possible sewing differences.

From solid cream, cut:
- 2—8½×95" appliqué border strips
- 2—8½×82" appliqué border strips
- 6—14" squares, cutting each diagonally twice in an X for a total of 24 triangles (there will be 2 left over)
- 20—10½" squares for appliqué foundations
- 10—9½" squares for setting
- 19—3½" squares
- 76—2×3½" rectangles
- 76—2" squares

From solid green, cut:
- 1—9×42" rectangle, cutting it into enough ⅝"-wide bias strips for sixty 5½"-long strips for stems (For specific instructions, see Cut Bias Strips in Quilter's Schoolhouse.)
- 40—2×3½" rectangles
- 40—2" squares
- 20 *each* of patterns A and A reversed
- 22 of Pattern G

From green print, cut:
- 4 of Pattern F
- 18 of Pattern E
- 20 of Pattern D
- 20—2" squares

From solid pink, cut:
- 1—27×42" rectangle, cutting it into enough 2½"-wide bias strips to total 390" in length for binding
- 40—2" squares
- 28 of Pattern B

From pink print, cut:
- 2—3¾×64¼" strips for outer border
- 2—3¾×77" strips for outer border
- 4 of Pattern H
- 20—2" squares
- 28 of Pattern C

From solid blue, cut:
- 27 of Pattern C
- 36—2×3½" rectangles
- 36—2" squares

From blue print, cut:
- 18—2" squares
- 27 of Pattern B
- 22 of Pattern D

From solid yellow, cut:
- 36—2" squares
- 27 of Pattern C

From yellow print, cut:
- 18—2" squares
- 27 of Pattern B

Assemble the Appliqué Blocks

1. For one appliqué block you'll need one solid cream 10½" square appliqué foundation, one green print D block corner, one solid green A leaf, one solid green A reversed leaf, three solid green ⅝×5½" bias stem strips, one blue print B tulip, one solid blue C tulip center, one solid pink B tulip, one pink print C tulip center, one yellow print B tulip, and one solid yellow C tulip center.

2. Fold the 10½" square appliqué foundation in half diagonally in both directions. Lightly finger-crease to create appliqué positioning guides.

3. Prepare the appliqué pieces, including the stem strips, by basting under the 3/16" seam allowances. Do not baste under seam allowances that will be covered by other pieces.

4. Referring to the Appliqué Block Assembly Diagram for placement, baste the stem strips onto the 10½" square appliqué foundation. Then pin the tulip, tulip center, and leaf pieces in place. To reduce bulk, trim the stems so that just ¼" runs under the tulip appliqués.

Appliqué Block Assembly Diagram

5. Using small slip stitches and threads that match the fabrics, appliqué the pieces in place, starting with the stems. Work from the bottom layer to the top layer.

6. Once the appliquéing is complete, trim the appliquéd foundation to 9½" square, including the seam allowances.

7. Place the Corner Cutting Template (found on *Pattern Sheet 2*) on the wrong side of the appliquéd foundation; align it in the corner where the stems end (see Diagram 1). Trace around the template, transferring reference marks. Carefully cut on the marked edge as shown in Diagram 2.

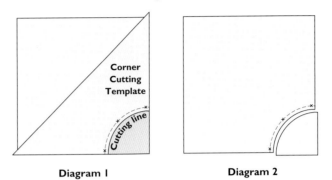

Diagram 1   **Diagram 2**

8. With right sides together, pin the appliquéd foundation to the green print D block corner, placing the first pin precisely at the center of the sewing line. Next place a pin at each end of the sewing line (see Diagram 3). Then pin the remainder of the seam until all reference marks are matched and the pieces fit together smoothly (see Diagram 4). (When pinning curved seams, use slender pins and pick up only a few threads at each position.) Sew together to complete an appliquéd block. The appliquéd block should still measure 9½" square, including seam allowances.

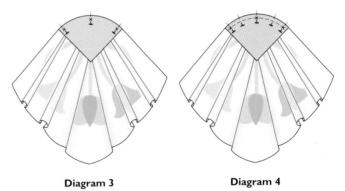

Diagram 3   **Diagram 4**

9. Repeat steps 1 through 8 to make a total of 20 appliquéd blocks.

Assemble the Patchwork Blocks

1. Referring to Diagram 5 on *page 140*, lay out two solid cream 2" squares, one solid blue 2" square, and one solid green 2" square in two rows. Sew together the squares in each row. Press the seam allowances in opposite directions. Then join the rows to make a Four-Patch Unit A. Press the seam

continued

allowance in one direction. The pieced Four-Patch unit should measure 3½" square, including the seam allowances. Repeat to make a second Four-Patch Unit A.

Diagram 5
Four-Patch Unit A

Diagram 6
Four-Patch Unit B

2. Using two solid pink 2" squares, one green print 2" square, and one pink print 2" square, repeat Step 1 to make one Four-Patch Unit B (see Diagram 6).

3. Using two solid yellow 2" squares, one yellow print 2" square, and one blue print 2" square, repeat Step 1 to make one Four-Patch Unit C (see Diagram 7).

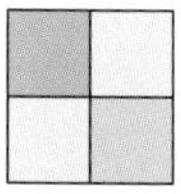

Diagram 7
Four-Patch Unit C

4. Referring to Diagram 8, sew together a solid cream 2×3½" rectangle and a solid green 2×3½" rectangle. Press the seam allowance toward the green rectangle. The pieced cream-and-green unit should measure 3½" square. Repeat to make a second cream-and-green unit.

Diagram 8 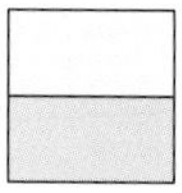   **Diagram 9**

5. Repeat Step 4, substituting a solid blue 2×3½" rectangle for the solid green to make two cream-and-blue units (see Diagram 9).

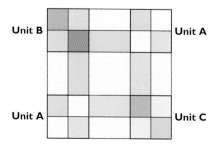

Unit B   Unit A

Unit A   Unit C

Block Assembly Diagram

6. Referring to the Block Assembly Diagram, lay out the eight pieced units and a solid cream 3½" square. Join the pieces in rows. Press the seam allowances in one direction, alternating directions with rows. Then join the rows to make a patchwork block. Press the seam allowances in one direction. The pieced patchwork block should measure 9½" square, including seam allowances.

7. Repeat steps 1 through 6 to make a total of 18 patchwork blocks.

Assemble the Center Block

1. Referring to Assemble the Patchwork Blocks, Step 1, use two solid cream 2" squares and two solid green 2" squares to make a Four-Patch Unit D (see Diagram 10). Repeat to make a second Four-Patch Unit D.

Diagram 10
Four-Patch Unit D

Diagram 11
Four-Patch Unit E

2. Using two solid pink 2" squares, one green print 2" square, and one pink print 2" square, make a Four-Patch Unit E (see Diagram 11). Repeat to make a second Four-Patch Unit E.

3. Referring to Assemble the Patchwork Blocks, Step 4, make a total of four cream-and-green units.

4. Referring to the Center Block Assembly Diagram, lay out the eight pieced units and a solid cream 3½" square. Join the pieces in rows. Press the seam allowances in each row in one direction, alternating directions with rows. Then join the rows to make the center patchwork block. Press the seam allowances in one direction. The pieced center patchwork block should measure 9½" square, including the seam allowances.

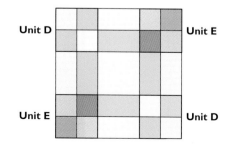

Unit D   Unit E

Unit E   Unit D

Center Block Assembly Diagram

Assemble the Setting Triangles

1. Place the Corner Cutting Template on the wrong side of a solid cream triangle; align it in the corner. Referring to Diagrams 1 and 2 on *page 139*, trace around the template, transferring reference marks; cut out.

2. Referring to Diagrams 3 and 4 on *page 139*, pin the cream triangle to a blue print D block corner; sew together to make a setting triangle. The pieced setting triangle should measure 9½" on two sides and 14" on one side, including the seam allowances.

3. Repeat to make a total of 22 pieced setting triangles.

Assemble the Quilt Center

Referring to the photograph on *page 138*, lay out the appliqué blocks, patchwork blocks, the 10 solid cream 9½" setting squares, and the pieced setting triangles in diagonal rows. Sew together the pieces in each row. Press the seam allowances in alternating directions. Then join the rows to make the quilt center. Press the seam allowances in one direction. The pieced quilt center should measure 64¼×77", including the seam allowances.

Add the Appliqué Border

With midpoints aligned, add a solid cream 8½×82" appliqué border strip to the top and bottom edges of the pieced quilt center and a solid cream 8½×95" appliqué border strip to each side edge of the pieced quilt center, mitering the corners. For information on mitering, see the Mitered Border Corner instructions in Quilter's Schoolhouse, which begins on *page 145*. Press the seam allowances toward the border.

Appliqué the Border

1. To appliqué the border, you'll need 18 green print E pieces, four green print F pieces, 22 solid green G pieces, seven solid blue C pieces, seven blue print B pieces, eight solid pink B pieces, eight pink print C pieces, seven solid yellow C pieces, and seven yellow print B pieces.

2. Prepare the pieces for appliqué by basting under the 3⁄16" seam allowances. Do not baste under edges that will be overlapped by other pieces.

3. Referring to the photograph on *page 138*, pin or hand-baste the appliqué pieces to the solid cream appliqué border.

4. Using small slip stitches and threads that match the fabrics, appliqué the pieces in place.

5. Place the Border Cutting Template (found on *Pattern Sheet 2*) in an appliquéd border corner on the right side of the quilt top. Trace around the template and carefully cut on the marked line (see Diagram 12). Repeat tracing and cutting in the other three corners.

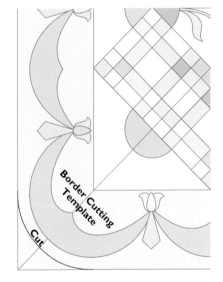

Diagram 12

Add the Outer Border

1. Sew the pink print 3¾×64¼" and 3¾×77" border strips together with the four of Pattern H to make the outer border (see Diagram 13).

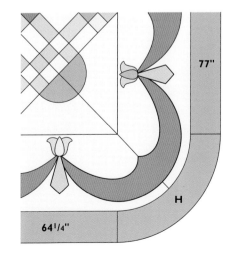

Diagram 13

continued

2. With right sides together and center marks aligned, pin the pink print outer border atop the cream appliquéd border. First pin the borders together along the straight edges, then pin at each end of the curves. Finish by pinning generously in between.

3. Join the borders, removing each pin just before your needle reaches it, to complete the quilt top. Press the seam allowance toward the cream border.

Complete the Quilt

1. Layer the quilt top, batting, and backing according to the instructions in Quilter's Schoolhouse, which begins on *page 145*. Quilt as desired.

2. Use the solid pink 2½"-wide bias strips to bind the quilt according to the instructions in Quilter's Schoolhouse.

WINDOW VALANCE

Follow the gentle curves of the

appliquéd swag design to create

a graceful window treatment.

Materials

20×70" rectangle of red check for valance

½ yard of green polka dot for appliqués

⅛ yard of green print for appliqués

Scraps of red floral for appliqués

½ yard of solid red for appliqués and binding

1 yard of fusing-adhesive material

Machine-embroidery thread in colors to match
   appliqués

Finished size: 15×69"

Cut the Fabrics

To make the best use of your fabrics, cut the pieces in the order that follows. *Note:* To make this project for an alternate window size, cut your valance fabric the necessary width, then adjust the number of appliquéd swags as desired.

This project uses "Bella Tulip Garden" patterns, which are on *Pattern Sheet 2*. To use fusing-adhesive material for appliquéing, as was done in this project, complete the following steps.

1. Lay the fusing-adhesive material, paper side up, over the patterns. Use a pencil to trace each pattern the specified number of times, leaving ½" between tracings. Cut out the pieces roughly ¼" outside of the traced lines.

2. Following the manufacturer's instructions, press the fusing-adhesive material shapes onto the backs of the designated fabrics; let cool. Cut out the shapes on the drawn lines. Peel off the paper backing.

From green polka dot, cut:
• 5 of Pattern E, cutting one in half

From green print, cut:
• 5 of Pattern G

From red floral, cut:
• 5 of Pattern B

From solid red, cut:
• 1—18" square, cutting it into enough 2"-wide bias strips to total 80" in length for binding (For specific instructions, see Cut Bias Strips, in Quilter's Schoolhouse, which begins on *page 145.*)
• 5 of Pattern C

Appliqué the Valance

1. Referring to the photograph *opposite* and the Valance Cutting Diagram, lay out the appliqué shapes on the red check 20×70" rectangle, beginning and ending with a half Pattern E; rearrange until you're pleased with the swag design.

2. Fuse the shapes in place following the manufacturer's instructions. Let the fabrics cool. Machine-satin-stitch the appliqué edges using matching threads.

Complete the Valance

1. Referring to the Valance Cutting Diagram, mark the lower edge of the valance, following the appliquéd swag design. Carefully cut on the marked line.

2. Turn each valance side edge under ¼" twice and press. Topstitch the folded side edges in place.

3. Turn under the valance top edge ¼" and press. Then fold it under 1½"; press. Topstitch ⅜" from the folded edge, then 1¼" from the first row of topstitching.

4. Use the solid red 2"-wide bias strips to bind the bottom valance edge according to the instructions in Quilter's Schoolhouse.

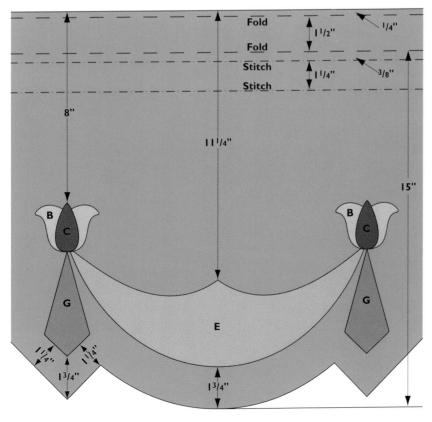

Valance Cutting Diagram

143

Bella Tulip Garden

EMBROIDERED TEA TOWEL

Create a redwork pattern using the appliqué

designs of "Bella Tulip Garden."

Materials

Striped linen tea towel

Red embroidery floss

Red fine-tip permanent marking pen

Tracing paper

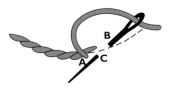

Stem Stitch

Embroider the Tea Towel

1. Referring to the photograph *above,* trace "Bella Tulip Garden" appliqué patterns A, B, and C on *Pattern Sheet 2* onto tracing paper to create the redwork design. Add two lines ¼" apart for each tulip stem, to complete the embroidery pattern.

2. Tape the embroidery pattern to a light box or sunny window. Position the tea towel over the pattern as desired; tape the towel in place. Trace the embroidery pattern onto the towel using a red fine-tip permanent marking pen.

3. Using a stem stitch and three strands of red embroidery floss, embroider the design.

   To stem-stitch, pull the needle up at A (see diagram at *left*). Insert the needle back into the fabric at B, about ⅜" away from A. Holding the thread out of the way, bring the needle back up at C and pull the thread through so it lies flat against the fabric. The distances between points A, B, and C should be equal. Pull with equal tautness after each stitch.

4. Press the towel from the wrong side when the embroidery is complete.

QUILTER'S SCHOOLHOUSE

GETTING STARTED

Before you begin any project, collect the tools and materials you'll need in one place. If you're an experienced sewer, you'll find you own some of the necessary equipment. Items adapted specifically for quilters are available in fabric and quilt stores.

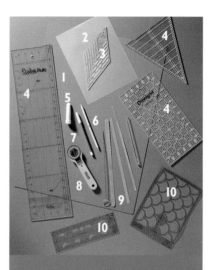

Basic Tools
1. Rotary cutting mat
2. Template plastic
3. Template
4. Acrylic rulers
5. Chalk marker
6. Marking pencil
7. Water-erasable marker
8. Rotary cutter
9. Bias bars
10. Quilting stencils

Tools

CUTTING

Acrylic ruler: For making perfectly straight cuts with a rotary cutter, choose a ruler of thick, clear plastic. Many sizes are available. A 6×24" ruler marked in ¼" increments with 30°, 45°, and 60° angles is a good first purchase.

Rotary cutter and mat: These tools have revolutionized quilting because a rotary cutter's round blade cuts strips, squares, triangles, and diamonds more quickly, efficiently, and accurately than scissors. A rotary cutter should always be used with a mat designed specifically for it. In addition to protecting the table, the mat helps keep the fabric from shifting while you cut.

Scissors: You'll need one pair for fabric and another for paper and plastic.

Pencils and other marking tools: Marks made with special quilt markers are easy to remove after sewing and quilting.

Template plastic: This slightly frosted plastic comes in sheets about ¹⁄₁₆" thick.

PIECING

Iron and ironing board: Pressing seams ensures accurate piecing.

Sewing thread: Use 100-percent-cotton thread.

Sewing machine: Any machine in good working order with well-adjusted tension will produce pucker-free patchwork seams.

APPLIQUÉ

Fusing-adhesive material: Instead of the traditional pinning method, secure cutout shapes to the background of an appliqué block with this iron-on adhesive.

Hand-sewing needles: For hand appliqué, most quilters like fine quilting needles.

HAND QUILTING

Frame or hoop: You'll get smaller, more even stitches if you stretch your quilt as you stitch. A frame supports the quilt's weight, ensures even tension, and frees both your hands for stitching. However, once set up, it cannot be disassembled until the quilting is complete. Hoops are more portable and less expensive. Quilting hoops are deeper than embroidery hoops to accommodate the thickness of quilt layers.

Quilting needles: A "between" or quilting needle is short with a small eye. Common sizes are 8, 9, and 10; size 8 is best for beginners.

Quilting thread: Quilting thread, including the preferred 100-percent-cotton variety, is stronger than sewing thread.

Thimble: This finger cover relieves the pressure required to push a needle through several layers of fabric and batting.

continued

MACHINE QUILTING

Darning foot: You may find this tool, also called a hopper foot, in your sewing machine's accessory kit. If not, have the model and brand of your machine available when you go to purchase one. It is used for free-motion stitching.

Safety pins: They hold the layers together during quilting.

Table or other large work surface that's level with your machine bed: Your quilt will need the support.

Thread: Use 100-percent-cotton quilting thread, cotton-wrapped polyester quilting thread, or very fine nylon monofilament thread.

Walking foot: This sewing-machine accessory helps you keep long, straight quilting lines smooth and pucker-free.

Choose Your Fabrics

It is no surprise that most quilters prefer 100-percent-cotton fabrics for quiltmaking. Cotton fabric minimizes seam distortion, presses crisply, and is easy to quilt. Most patterns, including those in this book, specify quantities for 44/45"-wide fabrics unless otherwise noted. Our projects call for a little extra yardage in length to allow for minor errors and slight shrinkage.

Prepare Your Fabrics

There are conflicting opinions about the need to prewash fabric. The debate is a modern one because most antique quilts were made with unwashed fabric. However, the dyes and sizing used today are unlike those used a century ago.

Prewashing fabric offers quilters certainty as its main advantage. Today's fabrics resist bleeding and shrinkage, but some of both can occur in some fabrics—an unpleasant prospect once you've assembled the quilt. Some quilters find prewashed fabric easier to quilt. If you choose to prewash your fabric, press it well before cutting.

Other quilters prefer the crispness of unwashed fabric for machine piecing. And, if you use fabrics with the same fiber content throughout the quilt, then any shrinkage that occurs in its first washing should be uniform. Some quilters find this small amount of shrinkage desirable, since it gives the quilt a slightly puckered, antique look.

We recommend you prewash a scrap of each fabric to test it for shrinkage and bleeding. If you choose to prewash a fabric, unfold it to a single layer. Wash it in warm water to allow the fabric to shrink and/or bleed. If the fabric bleeds,

rinse it until the water runs clear. Don't use any fabric in your quilt if it hasn't stopped bleeding. Hang fabric to dry, or tumble it in the dryer until slightly damp.

Select the Batting

For a small beginner project, a thin cotton batting is a good choice. It has a tendency to "stick" to fabric so it requires less basting. Also, it's easy to stitch. It's wise to follow the stitch density (distance between rows of stitching required to keep the batting from shifting and wadding up inside the quilt) recommendation printed on the packaging. Cotton batting is a good choice for garments because it shapes to the body.

Polyester batting is lightweight and readily available. In general, it springs back to its original height when compressed, adding a puffiness to quilts. It tends to "beard" (work out between the weave of the fabric) more than natural fibers. Polyester fleece is denser and works well for pillow tops and place mats.

Wool batting has good loft retention and absorbs moisture, making it ideal for cool, damp climates. Read the label carefully before purchasing a wool batting because it may require special handling.

CUTTING WITH TEMPLATES

A successful quilt requires precise cutting of pieces.

The traditional method employs scissors and patterns called

templates. It's the best way to cut curved pieces, and many quilters

enjoy it for other shapes too. Or, you can speed-cut squares,

rectangles, and triangles using the rotary techniques described

on pages 148 to 150.

About Scissors

Sharp scissor blades are vital to accurate cutting, but keeping them sharp is difficult because each use dulls the metal slightly. Cutting paper and plastic speeds the dulling process, so invest in a second pair for those materials and reserve your best scissors for fabric.

Make the Templates

For some quilts, you'll need to cut out the same shape multiple times. For accurate piecing later, the individual pieces should be identical to one another. The secret is in the templates.

A template is a pattern made from extra-sturdy material so you can trace around it many times without wearing away the edges. Acrylic templates for many common shapes are available at quilt shops. Or, you can make your own by duplicating printed patterns (like those on the Pattern Sheets) on plastic.

To make permanent templates, we recommend using easy-to-cut template plastic, available at crafts supply stores. This material lasts indefinitely, and its transparency allows you to trace the pattern directly onto its surface.

To make a template, lay the plastic over a printed pattern. Trace the pattern onto the plastic using a ruler and a permanent marker. This will ensure straight lines, accurate corners, and permanency. *Note:* If the pattern you are tracing is a half-pattern to begin with, you must first make a full-size pattern. To do so, fold a piece of tracing paper in half and crease; unfold. Lay the tracing paper over the half-pattern, aligning the crease with the fold line indicated on the pattern. Trace the half pattern. Then rotate the tracing paper, aligning the half pattern on the opposite side of the crease to trace the other half of the pattern. Use this full-size pattern to create your template.

For hand piecing and appliqué, make templates the exact size of the finished pieces, without seam allowances, by tracing the patterns' dashed lines. For machine piecing, make templates with the seam allowances included.

For easy reference, mark each template with its letter designation, grain line if noted, and block name. Verify the template's size by placing it over the printed pattern. Templates must be accurate or the error, however small, will compound many times as you assemble the quilt. To check the accuracy of your templates, make a test block before cutting the fabric pieces for an entire quilt.

Trace the Templates

To mark on fabric, use a pencil, white dressmaker's pencil, chalk, or a special quilt marker that makes a thin, accurate line. Do not use a ballpoint or ink pen that may bleed if washed. Test all marking tools on a fabric scrap before using them.

To trace pieces that will be used for hand piecing or appliqué, place templates facedown on the wrong side of the fabric and trace; position the tracings at least ½" apart (see Diagram 1, Template A). The lines drawn on the fabric are the sewing lines. Mark cutting lines, or estimate by eye a seam allowance around each piece as you cut out the pieces. For hand piecing, add a ¼" seam allowance when cutting out the pieces; for hand appliqué, add a ³⁄₁₆" seam allowance.

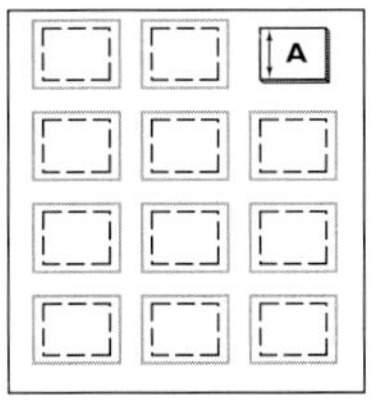

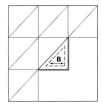

Diagram 1

Templates used to make pieces for machine piecing have seam allowances included so you can use common lines for efficient cutting. Place templates facedown on the wrong side of the fabric and trace; position them without space in between (see Diagram 2, Template B). Using sharp scissors or a rotary cutter and ruler, cut precisely on the drawn (cutting) lines.

Diagram 2

Templates for Angled Pieces

When two patchwork pieces come together and form an angled opening, a third piece must be set into this angle. This happens frequently when using diamond shapes.

For a design that requires setting in, a pinhole or window template makes it easy to mark the fabric with each shape's exact sewing and cutting lines and the exact point of each corner on

the sewing line. By matching the corners of adjacent pieces, you'll be able to sew them together easily and accurately.

To make a pinhole template, lay template plastic over a pattern piece. Trace both the cutting and sewing lines onto the plastic. Carefully cut out the template on the cutting line. Using a sewing-machine needle or any large needle, make a hole in the template at each corner on the sewing line (matching points). The holes must be large enough for a pencil point or other fabric marker to poke through.

To make a window template, lay the template plastic over a pattern piece. Trace both the cutting and sewing lines onto the plastic. Cut out the template on the cutting line. Then, with a crafts knife, cut on the sewing line, and remove the center of the template.

Trace Angled Pieces

To mark fabric using a pinhole template, lay it facedown on the wrong side of the fabric and trace. Using a pencil, mark dots on the fabric through the holes in the template to create matching points. Cut out the fabric piece on the drawn line, making sure the matching points are marked.

To mark fabric using a window template, lay it facedown on the wrong side of the fabric (see Diagram 3). With a marking tool, mark the cutting line, sewing line, and each corner on the sewing line (matching points). Cut out the fabric piece on the cutting lines, making sure all pieces have sewing lines and matching points marked.

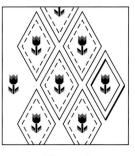

Diagram 3

ROTARY CUTTING

For many quilters, the thought of slicing through fabric with the quick roll of a razor-sharp blade is frightening. If you count yourself among those daunted by rotary cutting, fear not! We've taken the guesswork out of rotary cutting with this primer.

Successfully piecing a quilt top depends on careful, precise cutting. Inconsistency in the size of the pieces cut can magnify problems exponentially over the course of assembling an entire quilt top. One of the strongest appeals of rotary cutting is the precision and speed with which you can cut multiples of the same shape, thus bringing accuracy and enjoyment to the quiltmaking process.

That said, what can be done with the greatest of ease by the sales staff at the local quilt shop may look baffling to those who have always cut out strips, squares, triangles, and diamond-shape pieces with scissors, one at a time. Whether it's the equipment itself, the position of the ruler, or the way to read all those lines and hash marks on the ruler that's stopping you from giving it a try, take the time to review this primer. You'll learn how simple rotary cutting can be and how much time it can save you in cutting out your quilts.

Rotary-Cutting Tools Needed

There are three basic pieces of equipment needed—ruler, mat, and rotary cutter. While the tools come in many shapes, sizes, and styles, almost every brand can be used with success.

Acrylic ruler: For making perfectly straight cuts with a rotary cutter, choose a ruler of thick, clear plastic. Many sizes are available. A 6×24" ruler marked in ¼" increments with 30°, 45°, and 60° angles is a good first purchase. As you become more proficient at rotary cutting, you may wish to purchase additional acrylic rulers and templates in a variety of shapes and sizes.

Rotary-cutting mat: A rotary cutter should always be used with a mat designed specifically for it. In addition to protecting the table, the mat helps keep the fabric from shifting while you cut. Often these mats are described as self-healing, meaning the blade does not leave slash marks or grooves in the surface, even after repeated usage. While many shapes and styles are available, a 16×23" mat marked with a 1" grid, with hash marks at ⅛" increments and 45° and 60° angles is a good choice.

Cutting mats usually have one side with a printed grid and one plain side. To avoid confusion when lining up fabric with the preprinted lines on the ruler, some quilters prefer to work on the plain side of the mat. Others prefer to use the mat's grid. The choice is yours.

Rotary cutter: The round blade of a rotary cutter will cut up to six layers of fabric at once. Because the blade is so sharp, be sure to purchase one with a safety guard and keep the guard over the blade when you're not cutting. The blade can be removed from the handle and replaced when it gets dull. Commonly available in three sizes, a good first blade is a 45mm.

Plan for Cutting

Quilt-Lovers' Favorites™ instructions list pieces in the order in which they should be cut to make the best use of your fabrics. Always consider the fabric grain before cutting. The arrow on a pattern piece or template indicates which direction the fabric grain should run. One or more straight sides of the pattern piece or template should follow the fabric's lengthwise or crosswise grain.

The lengthwise grain, parallel to the selvage (the tightly finished edge), has the least amount of stretch. (Do not use the selvage of a woven fabric in a quilt. When washed, it may shrink more than the rest of the fabric.) Crosswise grain, perpendicular to the selvage, has a little more give. The edge of any pattern piece that will be on the outside of a block or quilt should always be cut on the lengthwise grain. Be sure to press the fabric before cutting to remove any wrinkles or folds.

Using a Rotary Cutter

When cutting, keep an even pressure on the rotary cutter and make sure the blade is touching the edge of the ruler. The less you move your fabric when cutting, the more accurate you'll be.

If your cutter doesn't cut through all the fabric layers, check the following:
• *Is the blade dull?* If so, change the blade and carefully dispose of the old one.
• *Is there a nick in the blade?* You'll know there's a nick by evenly spaced uncut spots, the result of the blade not touching the fabric each time it makes a complete rotation.
• *Did you put enough pressure on the rotary cutter?* If you've checked to make sure you don't have a dull blade, this may be the problem. Two telltale signs of this problem are areas along the cut edge where the fabric layers weren't cut through cleanly or where only the uppermost layers were cut through. First, try to apply more pressure when cutting. If the problem persists, you may have to cut through fewer layers at a time.

SQUARING UP THE FABRIC EDGE
Before rotary-cutting fabric into strips, it is imperative that one fabric edge be made straight, or squared up. Since all subsequent cuts will be measured from this straight edge, squaring up the fabric edge is an important step. There are several

different techniques for squaring up an edge, some of which involve the use of a pair of rulers. For clarity and simplicity, we have chosen to describe a single-ruler technique here. *Note:* The instructions as described are for right-handers.

1. Lay your fabric on the rotary mat with the right side down and one selvage edge away from you. Fold the fabric with the wrong side inside and the selvages together. Fold the fabric in half again, lining up the fold with the selvage edges. Lightly hand-crease all of the folds.

2. Position the folded fabric on the cutting mat with the selvage edges away from you and the bulk of the fabric length to your left. With the ruler on top of the fabric, align a horizontal grid line on the ruler with the lower folded fabric edge, leaving about 1" of fabric exposed along the right-hand edge of the ruler (see Photo 1). Do not worry about or try to align the uneven raw edges along the right-hand side of the fabric. *Note:* If the grid lines on the cutting mat interfere with your ability to focus on the ruler grid lines, turn your cutting mat over and work on the unmarked side.

3. Hold the ruler firmly in place with your left hand, keeping your fingers away from the right-hand edge and spreading your fingers apart slightly. Apply pressure to the ruler with your fingertips to prevent it from slipping as you cut. With the ruler firmly in place, hold the rotary cutter so the blade is touching the right-hand edge of the ruler. Roll the blade

along the ruler edge, beginning just off the folded edge and pushing the cutter away from you, toward the selvage edge.

4. The fabric strip to the right of the ruler's edge should be cut cleanly away, leaving you with a straight edge from which you can measure all subsequent cuts. Do not pick up the fabric once the edge is squared; instead, turn the cutting mat to rotate the fabric and begin cutting strips.

CUTTING AND SUBCUTTING STRIPS
To use a rotary cutter to its greatest advantage, first cut a strip of fabric, then subcut the strip into specific sizes. For example, if your instructions say to cut forty 2" squares, follow these steps.

1. First cut a 2"-wide strip crosswise on the fabric. Assuming you have squared up the fabric edge as described earlier, you can turn your cutting mat clockwise 180° with the newly squared-up edge on your left and the excess fabric on the right. Place the ruler on top of the fabric.

2. Align the 2" grid mark on the ruler with the squared-up edge of the fabric (see Photo 2). *Note:* Align only the vertical grid mark and the fabric raw edge; ignore the selvages at the lower edge that may not line up perfectly with the horizontal ruler grid. A good rule of thumb to remember when rotary-cutting fabric is "the piece you want to keep should be under the ruler." That way, if you accidentally swerve away from the ruler when cutting, the piece under the ruler will be "safe."

3. Placing your rotary cutter along the ruler's right-hand edge and holding the ruler firmly with your left hand, run the blade along the ruler, as in Step 3 of Squaring Up the Fabric Edge, *left,* to cut the strip. Remove the ruler.

4. Sliding the excess fabric out of the way, carefully turn the 2" strip so it is horizontal on the mat. Refer to Squaring Up the Fabric Edge to trim off the selvage edges, squaring up those fabric ends.

5. Then align the 2" grid mark on the ruler with the squared-up edge of the fabric (the 2" square you want to keep is under the ruler). Hold the ruler with your left hand and run the rotary cutter along the right-hand ruler edge to cut a 2" square. You can cut multiple 2" squares from one strip by sliding the ruler over 2" from the previous cutting line and cutting again (see Photo 3). From a 44/45" strip, you'll likely be able to cut twenty-one 2" squares. Since in this example you need a total of 40, cut a second 2"-wide strip and subcut it into 2" squares.

CUTTING TRIANGLES
Right triangles also can be quickly and accurately cut with a rotary cutter. There are two common ways to cut triangles. An example of each method follows.

To cut two triangles from one square, the instructions in *American Patchwork & Quilting* may read:

From green print, cut:
- 20—3" squares, cutting each in half diagonally for a total of 40 triangles

continued

1. Referring to Cutting and Subcutting Strips, on *page 149,* cut a 3"-wide fabric strip and subcut the strip into 3" squares.

2. Line up the ruler's edge with opposite corners of the triangle to cut it in half diagonally (see Photo 4). Cut along the ruler's edge. *Note:* The triangle's resultant long edges are on the bias. Avoid stretching or overhandling these edges when piecing so that seams don't become wavy and distorted.

To cut four triangles from one square, the instructions may read:

From green print, cut:
- 20—6" squares, cutting each diagonally twice in an X for a total of 80 triangles

3. Referring to Cutting and Subcutting Strips on *page 149,* cut a 6"-wide fabric strip and subcut it into 6" squares.

4. Line up the ruler's edge with opposite corners of the triangle to cut it in half diagonally. Cut along the ruler's edge; do not separate the two triangles created. Line up the ruler's edge with the remaining corners and cut to make a total of four triangles (see Photo 5). *Note:* The triangle's resultant short edges are on the bias. Avoid stretching or overhandling these edges when piecing so that seams don't become wavy and distorted.

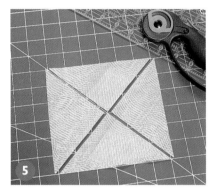

Practice Brings Confidence

Now that you've reviewed the basics of rotary cutting, practice your skills with a project from this book. All the projects in Chapter 2, "Simple Sensations," are designed to be rotary-cut. As with all techniques, the more you work with your rotary cutter, the easier and more natural the cutting movement will become. The time you save in cutting can be used to do more piecing and quilting!

PIECING

Patchwork piecing consists of sewing fabric pieces together in a specific pattern. There are several approaches to piecing a quilt. Understanding them helps you choose the one you'll enjoy most.

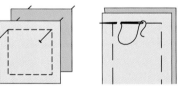

Diagram 1   **Diagram 2**

Diagram 3

Hand Piecing

In hand piecing, seams are sewn only on the marked sewing lines rather than from one raw edge to the other. Begin by matching the edges of two pieces with the right sides of the fabrics together. Sewing lines should be marked on the wrong side of both pieces. Push a pin through both fabric layers at each corner (see Diagram 1). Secure the pins perpendicular to the sewing line. Insert more pins between the corners.

Insert a needle through both fabrics at the seam-line corner. Make one or two backstitches atop the first stitch to secure the thread. Weave the needle in and out of the fabric along the seam line, taking four to six tiny stitches at a time before you pull the thread taut (see Diagram 2). Remove the pins as you sew. Turn the work over occasionally to see that the stitching follows the marked sewing line on the other side.

Sew eight to 10 stitches per inch along the seam line. At the end of the seam, remove the last pin and make the ending stitch through the hole left by the corner pin. Backstitch over the last stitch and end the seam with a loop knot (see Diagram 3).

To join rows of patchwork by hand, hold the sewn pieces with right sides together and seams matching. Insert pins at corners of the matching pieces. Add additional pins as necessary, securing each pin perpendicular to the sewing line (see Diagram 4).

Stitch the joining seam as before, but do not sew across the seam allowances that join the patches. At each seam allowance, make a

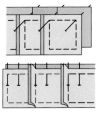

Diagram 4

backstitch or loop knot, then slide the needle through the seam allowance. (see Diagram 5). Knot or backstitch again to give the intersection strength, then sew the remainder of the seam. Press each seam as it is completed.

Diagram 5

Machine Piecing

Machine piecing depends on sewing an exact ¼" seam allowance. Some machines have a presser foot that is the proper width, or a ¼" foot is available. To check the width of a machine's presser foot, sew a sample seam, with the raw fabric edges aligned with the right edge of the presser foot; measure the resultant seam allowance using graph paper with a ¼" grid.

If the presser foot does not indicate ¼", mark the distance on the throat plate with the aid of graph paper. Carefully trim graph paper along a grid line. Place the trimmed graph paper under the needle. Slowly lower the needle into the grid one line from the newly trimmed edge (see Diagram 6). Use masking tape to mark the new seam guide's location ahead of the needle.

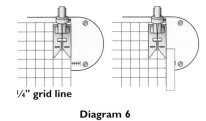

¼" grid line

Diagram 6

To test your newly marked seam guide, cut three 1½"-wide strips of different fabric scraps. Sew together two of the strips. Join the third strip.

Press the seam allowances away from the center. If your seam is ¼" wide, the center strip should measure 1" (see Diagram 7). If not, adjust your seam guide.

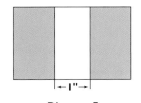

← 1" →

Diagram 7

Choosing Thread Color

Using two different thread colors—one on top of the machine and one in the bobbin—can help you to better match your thread color to your fabrics. If your quilt has many fabrics, use a neutral color, such as gray or beige, for both the top and bobbin threads throughout the quilt.

Chain Piecing

In machine piecing, squares and triangles in blocks should be sewn together from edge to edge. Save time and thread by chain-piecing whenever possible. To chain-piece, feed the pieces under the machine needle without lifting the presser foot or clipping the thread. The stitched patches will be linked by short lengths of thread; clip the threads to cut them apart.

Press for Success

In quilting, almost every seam needs to be pressed before the piece is sewn to another, so keep your iron and ironing board near your sewing area. It's important to remember to press with an up and down motion. Moving the iron around on the fabric can distort seams, especially those sewn on the bias.

Project instructions in this book generally tell you in what direction to press each seam. When in doubt, press both seam allowances toward the darker fabric. When joining rows of blocks, alternate the direction the seam allowances are pressed to ensure flat corners.

Setting in Pieces

The key to sewing angled pieces together is aligning marked matching points carefully. Whether you're stitching by machine or hand, start and stop sewing precisely at the matching points (see the dots in Diagram 8, top) and backstitch to secure the ends of the seams. This prepares the angle for the next piece to be set in.

Join two diamond pieces, sewing between matching points to make an angled unit (see Diagram 8).

Follow the specific instructions for either machine or hand piecing to complete the set-in seam.

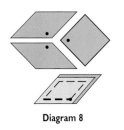

Diagram 8

Machine Piecing

With right sides together, pin one piece of the angled unit to one edge of the square (see Diagram 9). Match the seam's matching points by pushing a pin through both fabric layers to check the alignment. Machine-stitch the seam between the matching points. Backstitch to secure the ends of the seam; do not stitch into the ¼" seam allowance. Remove the unit from the sewing machine.

Bring the adjacent edge of the angled unit up and align it with the next edge of the square (see Diagram 10). Insert a pin in each corner to align matching points, then pin the remainder of the seam. Machine-stitch between matching points as before. Press the seam allowances of the set-in piece away from it.

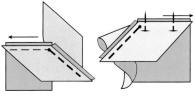

Diagram 9   **Diagram 10**

continued

Hand Piecing

Pin one piece of the angled unit to one edge of the square with right sides together (see Diagram 11). Use pins to align matching points at the corners.

Hand-sew the seam from the open end of the angle into the corner. Remove pins as you sew between matching points. Backstitch at the corner to secure stitches. Do not sew into the ¼" seam allowance and do not cut your thread.

Bring the adjacent edge of the square up and align it with the other edge of the angled unit. Insert a pin in each corner to align matching points, then pin the remainder of the seam (see Diagram 12). Hand-sew the seam from the corner to the open end of the angle, removing pins as you sew. Press the seam allowances of the set-in piece away from it.

Mitered Border Corners

A border surrounds the piecework of many quilts. Angled, mitered corners add to a border's framed effect.

To add a border with mitered corners, first pin a border strip to a quilt top edge, matching the center of the strip and the center of the quilt top edge. Sew together, beginning and ending the seam ¼" from the quilt top corners (see Diagram 13). Allow excess border fabric to extend beyond the edges. Repeat with remaining border strips. Press the seam allowances toward the border strips.

Overlap the border strips at each corner (see Diagram 14). Align the edge of a 90° right triangle with the raw edge of a top border strip so the long edge of the triangle intersects the seam in the corner. With a pencil, draw along the edge of the triangle

from the border seam out to the raw edge. Place the bottom border strip on top and repeat the marking process.

With the right sides of adjacent border strips together, match the marked seam lines and pin (see Diagram 15).

Beginning with a backstitch at the inside corner, stitch exactly on the marked lines to the outside edges of the border strips. Check the right side of the corner to see that it lies flat. Then trim the excess fabric, leaving a ¼" seam allowance. Press the seam open. Mark and sew the remaining corners in this manner.

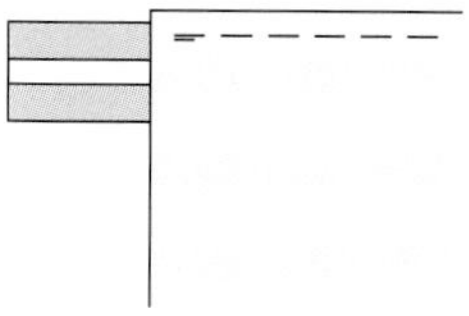

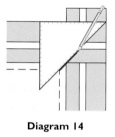

Diagram 14

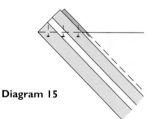

Diagram 15

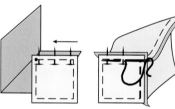

Diagram 11   **Diagram 12**

Diagram 13

APPLIQUÉ

With appliqué, you create a picture by stitching fabric shapes atop a foundation block.

Many techniques can be used to accomplish this, including traditional needle-turn appliqué,

fusible appliqué, and machine appliqué.

Start Simple

We encourage beginners to select an appliqué design with straight lines and gentle curves. Learning to make sharp points and tiny stitches takes practice.

In the following instructions, we've used a stemmed flower motif as the appliqué example.

Baste the Seam Allowances

Begin by turning under the appliqué piece ³⁄₁₆" seam allowances; press. Some quilters like to thread-baste the folded edges to ensure proper placement. Edges that will be covered by other pieces don't need to be turned under.

For sharp points on tips, trim the seam allowance to within ⅛" of the

stitching line (see Photo 1); taper the sides gradually to ³⁄₁₆". Fold under the seam allowance remaining on the tips. Then turn the seam allowances under on both sides of the tips. The side seam allowances will overlap slightly at the tips, forming sharp points. Baste the folded edges in place (see Photo 2). The turned seam allowances may form little pleats on the back side that you also should baste in place. You'll remove the basting stitches after the shape has been appliquéd to the foundation.

Make Bias Stems

In order to curve gracefully, appliqué stems are cut on the bias. The strips for stems can be prepared in two ways. You can fold and press the strip in thirds as shown in Photo 3. Or you can fold the bias strip in half lengthwise with the wrong side inside; press. Stitch ¼" in from the raw edges to keep them aligned. Fold the strip in half again, hiding the raw edges behind the first folded edge; press.

Position and Stitch

Pin the prepared appliqué pieces in place on the foundation using the position markings or referring to the block assembly diagram (see Photo 4). If your pattern suggests it, mark the position for each piece on the foundation block before you begin. Overlap the flowers and stems as indicated.

Using thread in colors that match the fabrics, sew each stem and blossom onto the foundation with small slip stitches as shown in Photo 5. (For photographic purposes, the thread color does not match the lily.)

Catch only a few threads of the stem or flower fold with each stitch. Pull the stitches taut but not so tight that they pucker the fabric. You can use the needle's point to manipulate the appliqué edges as needed. Take an extra slip stitch at the point of a petal to secure it to the foundation.

You can use hand-quilting needles for appliqué stitching, but some quilters prefer a longer milliner's or straw needle. The extra needle length aids in tucking fabric under before taking slip stitches.

If the foundation fabric shows through the appliqué fabrics, cut away the foundation fabric. Trimming the foundation fabric also reduces the bulk of multiple layers when quilting. Carefully trim the underlying fabric to within ¼" of the appliqué stitches (see Photo 6). Do not cut the appliqué fabric.

Double Appliqué

To ease the challenge of turning curved edges, many quilters prefer to face appliqué pieces. For this, trace each template onto the wrong side of the fabric. Cut out, leaving a ¼" seam allowance around all of the edges.

Place the cut piece, right side down, on a piece of sheer, nonfusible, nonwoven interfacing. Sew all the way around on the drawn line. Trim the interfacing slightly smaller than the fabric and clip inner curves.

Make a small clip in the center of the interfacing (see Diagram 1). Turn the appliqué right side out through the clipped opening. Press the piece from the fabric side, making sure no interfacing shows at the edges.

Diagram 1

Fusible Appliqué

For quick-finish appliqué, use paper-backed fusing-adhesive material. Then you can iron the shapes onto the foundation and add decorative stitching to the edges. This product consists of two layers, a fusible webbing lightly bonded to paper that peels off. The webbing adds a slight stiffness to the back of the appliqué pieces.

When you purchase this product, read the directions on the bolt end or packaging to make sure you're buying the right kind for your project. Some brands are specifically engineered to bond fabrics with no sewing at all. If you try to stitch fabric after it has bonded with one of these products, you may encounter difficulty. Some paper-backed fusible products are made exclusively for sewn edges; others work with or without stitching.

If you buy paper-backed fusing-adhesive material from a bolt, be sure fusing instructions are included because the iron temperature and timing varies by brand. This information is usually on the paper backing.

continued

With any of these products, the general procedure is to trace the pattern wrong side up onto the paper side of the fusing-adhesive material. Then place the fusing-adhesive material on the wrong side of the appliqué fabrics, paper side up, and use an iron to fuse the layers together. Then cut out the shapes, peel off the paper, turn the fabrics right side up, and fuse the shapes to the foundation fabric.

You also can fuse the fusing-adhesive material and fabric together before tracing. You'll still need to trace templates wrong side up on the paper backing.

If you've used a no-sew fusing-adhesive material, your appliqué is done. If not, there are several appealing ways to finish the edges of appliqué with stitching.

Blanket Stitch

This book's patterns often specify hand-worked blanket stitches (see Photo 7).

Using embroidery floss in a color that coordinates with the fabric color, pull the needle up at A, form a reverse L shape with the floss, and hold the angle of the L shape in place with your thumb. Push the needle down at B and come up at C to secure the stitch. Repeat the steps until you've stitched around the piece (see Diagram 2).

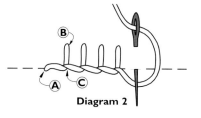

Diagram 2

Machine Stitches

The sewing machine offers several other decorative options. To simply secure the edges, standard zigzag stitches provide a neat finish. Using matching or contrasting thread produces distinctly different looks. For invisibility, use a hem stitch that consists of three or four straight stitches followed by a V stitch. Keep the straight stitches on the foundation and catch the appliquéd shape with the V. To dramatize appliquéd shapes, try a satin stitch (see Photo 8) or other decorative stitches worked in a contrasting thread.

QUILTING

A quilt top becomes a finished quilt when stitched to batting and backing.

The layers can be secured by hand, machine, or tying. Choose a method that harmonizes

with your quilt's design and intended use.

Choosing a Quilting Design

After you decide whether to hand- or machine-stitch, you still have decisions to make about the design you'll stitch in the quilt top.
Background fillers are simple designs in the open spaces. Most background fillers are patterns of straight lines, such as single or closely spaced double lines stitched vertically, horizontally, or diagonally. Crossed stitching lines make square or diamond grids.
Freestyle designs are meandering, allover patterns. Machine quilters refer to the technique as stippling.
Echo quilting is multiple lines of stitching that follow the outline of an appliqué or other design element, echoing its shape.
Quilting in the ditch is stitching close to the seam line on the side that does not have seam allowances. These stitches are more subtle than outline quilting (see photograph *opposite*) because they tend to disappear into seam lines.
Outline quilting stitches are made ¼" from the seam lines, just past the extra thickness of the pressed seam.

Mark the Design

Freestyle, outline, and in-the-ditch quilting do not require marking on the quilt top. For other designs, you'll need to mark the top, tracing a stencil, template, or drawing.

Before you begin, press the quilt top. Be sure to test your marker to make sure it shows up on the fabric and is easy to remove when finished.

Secure the template on a flat surface with masking tape. Match the quilt top seams with the edge guides of the pattern (see Photo 1). Firmly secure the quilt top over the template with masking tape.

Begin marking at the center of the quilt top and work toward the borders (see Photo 2). Mark the larger and/or more complex designs first, then fill in the smaller details. Mark

Background Filler   **Echo Quilting**   **Outline Quilting**

Quilting Template   **In the Ditch Quilting**

To end stitching, wind the thread twice around the needle close to the top, making a French knot. Then run the needle through the top and batting; bring it out a few inches away from the stitching. Hold the thread taut, clip it close to the top, and release it; the thread end will snap out of sight.

Quilting Stitches

Hand quilting takes practice. To begin, hold the needle between your thumb and index finger. Place your other hand under the quilt, with the tip of your index finger on the spot where the needle will come through the quilt back. With the needle angled slightly away from you, push the needle through the layers until you feel the tip of the needle beneath the quilt (see Photo 4 on *page 156*).

When you feel the needle tip, slide your finger underneath the quilt toward you, pushing against the side of the needle to help return it to the top. At the same time, with your top hand, roll the needle away from you. Gently push the needle forward and

the background filler last, if you choose to stitch one. Use a ruler to draw straight lines.

Baste the Layers

Properly assembling a quilt's layers ensures a smooth, wrinkle-free surface for quilting. Cut or piece the backing fabric so it is at least 3" larger on all sides than the quilt top. Fluff batting in a clothes dryer for a few minutes on an air-dry setting to remove wrinkles. Trim the batting so it is 3" larger all around than the quilt top.

Tape the backing to a smooth work surface, wrong side up. Center the batting atop the backing, smoothing it flat; tape or pin them together at the edges. Center the quilt top on the batting.

Baste the three layers together by stitching a horizontal and vertical line through the center to form quadrants on the quilt top. The basting stitches should be about 2" long and 4" apart (see Photo 3). If you will be lap-quilting, make the basting stitches

closer together since the quilt will be handled more. If you will be machine-quilting, you may substitute No. 1 safety pins for basting, pinning through all layers in the same pattern.

Hand Quilting

Viewed as the traditional method, hand quilting can take more time than piecing the top. Some stitchers like to hold the quilt loosely in their laps. Most feel, however, that straighter, smaller stitches are achieved if the work is held taut in a hoop or frame.

Stitch with about 18" of thread in your needle; knot one end. No knots should show on the front or back of a hand-quilted piece. To bury a knot inside the quilt, insert the needle through the top and the batting (but not the backing), a few inches away from the quilting area. Bring the needle back to the surface in position to make the first stitch. Gently tug on the thread, just enough to pop the knot through the top fabric and embed it in the batting.

continued

Repeat this rock-and-roll motion until the needle is full. Then pull it away from the quilt top until the stitches are snug. Remember that uniformity of stitching is more important than size.

Machine Quilting

Quilting by machine is more than 100 years old, but until recent years it was considered a less-desirable means of finishing a fine quilt. Today, improved sewing machines and presser feet make it possible to create heirloom-quality quilts in hours instead of months.

Before you're even ready to practice, make sure your machine is in top working order and its tension is reliable. Clean and oil it before you begin. Clear the lint from the bobbin area after each empty bobbin and lightly oil the race, shuttle, and any other moving parts with a cotton swab or telescoping oil bottle. Clean the entire machine again after eight hours of sewing.

Set up a work space that provides a large, flat surface level with the machine's bed (throat plate) to keep the quilt well supported and flat. If possible, set up one table behind the machine and another to your left. Try to arrange the work space so the machine faces into a room and the quilt doesn't have to climb the wall.

Finally, choose a comfortable chair that allows you to look down on your work. This lets your arms relax at your sides instead of reaching.

Straight Lines

To quilt long lines, such as in the ditch and grids, use a walking foot (see Photo 8). (Designs with curves and corners require the free-motion technique described at right.) If you've never machine-quilted, start with a practice piece, such as a single block of simple squares or strips. Layer it with a thin cotton batting and a muslin backing; baste with safety pins.

Rather than backstitching, lock off stitches by setting the machine's stitch length to the shortest setting. Start the line on that setting, sewing forward about ¼". Then stop and reset the

stitch length to 10 to 12 stitches per inch. Repeat this process at the beginning and end of every seam.

When working with a walking foot, start by sewing in the ditch of the quilt's lengthwise center seam, border to border. Turn the quilt crosswise, readjust the layers, and stitch the center crosswise seam. For small pieces, stitch all the lengthwise lines on one side of the center, then on the other side. Rotate the quilt and stitch the crosswise lines in the same manner.

For a large quilt, stitch all the lengthwise lines in the quadrant to the right of the lengthwise center seam. Turn the quilt 180° and stitch the lines in the diagonally opposite quadrant. Repeat the process in the remaining quadrants. Complete the grid by stitching crosswise lines in the same quadrant-by-quadrant order.

As you feed the fabric up to the walking foot, don't allow the foot to push fabric ahead. This causes tucks at the crossing of each seam. Give excess fabric to the foot, and allow it to ease the fabric into the seam evenly. Do not stretch or force the quilt top, as the batting and the finished quilt may become distorted.

Free-Motion Quilting

Quilting with a walking foot is limited to straight lines. For curved patterns, including hand quilters' fancy designs, use a darning foot (see Photo 9).

up through the quilt layers, until the amount of needle showing is the length you want the next stitch to be (see Photo 5).

Lift the eye of the needle with your thimble finger, positioning your thumb just ahead of the stitching. Rock the needle upward until it is almost perpendicular to the quilt top (see Photo 6). Push down on the needle until you feel the tip beneath the quilt again.

Push the needle tip up to the top with your finger underneath the quilt and, at the same time, with your thimble finger, roll the eye of the needle down and forward to return the tip to the surface (see Photo 7).

This foot jumps up and down as the needle raises and lowers, allowing you to move the fabric freely while the needle is up, but holding the layers flat and compressed when the needle is taking a stitch.

Drop or cover the machine's feed dogs. You will manually control the stitch length, direction, and speed at which the fabric moves.

For practice, layer a piece of thin cotton batting between two pieces of muslin. Bring the bobbin thread to the surface of the fabric and hold both threads as you begin to stitch. When you press on the foot control, however, the fabric will stand still. You need to manually move it in the direction you wish to go. The speed you run the machine combined with the speed you move the fabric creates your stitch length. Practice to get a feel for this and to develop a consistent stitch length.

In the beginning, move the fabric slowly while running the machine at a medium-fast speed. Try to develop a rhythm with the motor while making scribbles on the fabric. Rather than turning the fabric, glide it in the direction it needs to go. Practice locking your stitches by moving the fabric very slowly, which creates minute stitches, for about ¼". This should be done at the beginning and end of every quilting line.

Once you've practiced for a while, select a small project to machine-quilt. A print fabric top will camouflage small glitches. Outline, echo, and stippling are good first project patterns. Stippling is a meandering, allover technique involving lines that do not touch, do not cross, do not have points, and are consistently spaced. Look beyond the hole in the darning foot and watch where you've been and where you are going.

Fancier patterns, such as feathers and cables, require advance planning to minimize the number of endings. When you're ready to tackle those patterns, stop at a quilt shop for a reference book.

COVERED CORDING

Finish pillows and quilts with easy, tailored cording.

Covered cording is made by sewing a bias-cut fabric strip around a length of cording. The width of the bias strip will vary depending on the diameter of your cording. Refer to the specific project instructions for those measurements. Regardless, the method used to cover the cording is the same.

With the wrong side inside, fold under 1½" at one end of the bias strip. With the wrong side inside, fold the strip in half lengthwise to make the cording cover. Insert the cording next to the folded edge, placing a cording end 1" from the cording cover folded end. Using a machine cording foot, sew through both fabric layers right next to the cording (see Diagram 1).

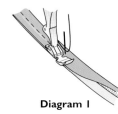

Diagram I

When attaching the cording to your project, begin stitching 1½" from the covered cording's folded end. Round the corners slightly, making sure the corner curves match. As you stitch

each corner, gently ease the covered cording into place (see Diagram 2).

After going around the entire edge of the project, cut the end of the cording so that it will fit snugly into the folded opening at the beginning (see Diagram 3). The ends of the cording should abut inside the covering. Stitch the ends in place to secure (see Diagram 4).

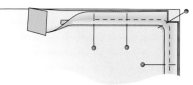

Diagram 2

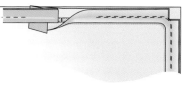

Diagram 3

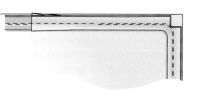

Diagram 4

CUTTING BIAS STRIPS

Strips for curved appliqué pattern pieces, such as meandering vines, and for binding curved edges should be cut on the bias (diagonally across the grain of a woven fabric), which runs at a 45° angle to the selvage and has the most give or stretch.

To cut bias strips, begin with a fabric square or rectangle. Use a large acrylic ruler to square up the left edge of the fabric. Make the first cut at a 45° angle to the left edge (see Bias Strip Diagram). Handle the

diagonal edges carefully to avoid distorting the bias. To cut a strip, measure the desired width parallel to the 45° cut edge; cut. Continue cutting enough strips to total the length needed.

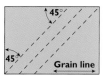

Bias Strip Diagram

HANGING SLEEVES

When you want a favorite quilt to become wall art,

hang it with care to avoid sagging, tearing, and wavy edges.

Quilts make wonderful pieces of wall art. When treated as museum pieces and hung properly, they won't deteriorate. Let size be your guide when determining how to hang your quilt.

Hang smaller quilts, a 25" square or less, with purchased clips, sewn-on tabs, or pins applied to the corners. Larger quilts require a hanging sleeve attached to the back. It may take a few minutes more to sew on a sleeve, but the effort preserves your hours of work with less distortion and damage.

Make a Hanging Sleeve

1. Measure the quilt's top edge.

2. Cut a 6"- to 10"-wide strip of prewashed fabric 2" longer than the quilt's top edge. For example, if the top edge is 40", cut a 6×42" strip. A 6"-wide strip is sufficient for a dowel or drapery rod. If you're using something bigger in diameter, cut a wider fabric strip. If you're sending your quilt to be displayed at a quilt show, adjust your measurements to accommodate the show's requirements.

3. Fold under 1½" on both short ends of the fabric strip. Sew ¼" from raw edges (see Diagram 1).

Diagram I

Diagram 2

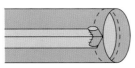

Diagram 3

4. Fold the fabric strip in half lengthwise with the wrong side inside; pin. Stitch together the long edges with a ¼" seam allowance (see Diagram 2) to make the sleeve. Press the seam allowance open and center the seam in the middle of the sleeve (see Diagram 3).

5. Center the sleeve on the quilt backing about 1" below the binding with the seam facing the backing (see Diagram 4). Stitching through the backing and batting, slip-stitch the sleeve to the quilt along both long edges and the portions of the short edges that touch the backing.

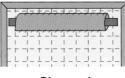

Diagram 4

6. Slide a wooden dowel or slender piece of wood that is 1" longer than the finished sleeve into the sleeve and hang as desired.

Slip in a Sleeve

If you decide early enough to include a hanging sleeve, another option is to sew one edge of the sleeve to the quilt backing with your binding.

1. Sew together your quilt as directed up to the point of attaching the binding.

2. Measure the quilt's top edge.

3. Cut a 6"- to 10"-wide strip of prewashed fabric 2" longer than the quilt's top edge.

4. Fold under 1½" on both short ends of the fabric strip. Sew 1¼" from each folded edge (see Diagram 1).

5. Fold the fabric strip in half lengthwise with the wrong side inside; pin. Stitch together the long edges with a ¼" seam allowance (see Diagram 2) to make the sleeve; do not press the seam allowance open.

6. Line up the long edges of the sleeve with the top raw edge of the quilt backing. Pin sleeve and binding in place at the same time. Sew the binding to quilt top using a slightly less than ¼" seam allowance to accommodate the sleeve. Slip-stitch the binding, then the long folded edge of the sleeve to the quilt backing.

Use Multiple Sleeves

For quilts 35" square or less you can use multiple fabric loops rather than a full sleeve.

1. Cut several 3½×5½" rectangles of fabric. Turn each rectangle's long edges under ¼"; press. Stitch ⅛" from the folded edges. Repeat with the short edges of the rectangles.

2. Evenly space the hemmed rectangles across the quilt backing 1" from the bottom edge of the binding. Slip-stitch the rectangles in place (see Diagram 5).

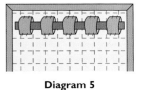

Diagram 5

For even larger quilts (a hanging edge of 60" to 70"), you can make two or three sleeve sections. This lets you use more nails or brackets and evenly distributes the quilt's weight.

For example, to make three sleeves, measure the quilt's top edge and divide by 3. Add 2" to the new measurement. Cut three fabric pieces this length and make the sleeves as previously instructed. (If your quilt is 96" square, divide 96" by 3 to get 32"; add 2" to 32" for a length for 34". Cut three 6×34" strips.)

FINISHING

The final step in quiltmaking is to bind the edges.

Follow our easy instructions for a neat and durable edge on your quilt.

Binding

The binding for most quilts is cut on the straight grain of the fabric. If your quilt has curved edges, cut the strips on the bias (see *page 157*). The cutting instructions for projects in this book specify the number of binding strips or a total length needed to finish the quilt. The instructions also specify enough width for a French-fold or double-layer binding because it's easier to apply and adds durability.

Join the strips with diagonal seams to make one continuous binding strip (see Diagram 1). Trim the excess fabric, leaving ¼" seam allowances. Press the seam allowances open. Then, with the wrong sides together, fold under 1" at one end of the binding strip (see Diagram 2); press. Fold the strip in half lengthwise (see Diagram 3); press.

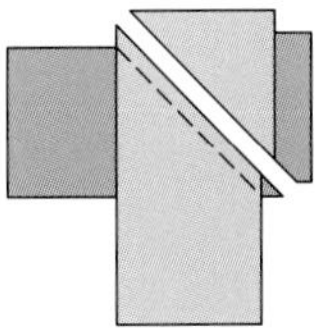

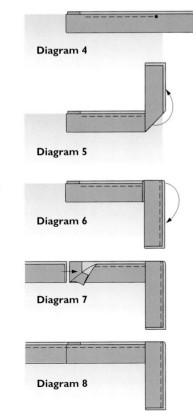

Diagram I

Diagram 2

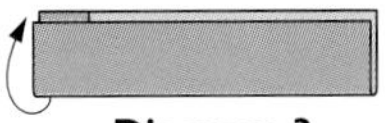

Diagram 3

Beginning in the center of one side, place the binding strip against the right side of the quilt top, aligning the binding strip's raw edges with the quilt top's raw edge (see Diagram 4). Beginning 1½" from the folded edge, sew through all layers, stopping ¼" from the corner. Backstitch, then clip the threads. Remove the quilt from under the sewing-machine presser foot.

Fold the binding strip upward (see Diagram 5), creating a diagonal fold, and finger-press.

Holding the diagonal fold in place with your finger, bring the binding strip down in line with the next edge, making a horizontal fold that aligns with the top edge of the quilt (see Diagram 6).

Start sewing again at the top of the horizontal fold, stitching through all layers. Sew around the quilt, turning each corner in the same manner.

When you return to the starting point, lap the binding strip inside the beginning fold (see Diagram 7). Finish sewing to the starting point (see Diagram 8). Trim the batting and backing fabric even with the quilt top edges.

Turn the binding over the edge of the quilt to the back. Hand-stitch the binding to the backing fabric, making sure to cover any machine stitching.

To make mitered corners on the back, hand-stitch the binding up to a corner; fold a miter in the binding. Take a stitch or two in the fold to secure it. Then stitch the binding in

Diagram 4

Diagram 5

Diagram 6

Diagram 7

Diagram 8

place up to the next corner. Finish each corner in the same manner.

Tying a Quilt

Tying, or tufting, is a quick-and-easy alternative to quilting. It is an appropriate, useful finish for a quilt that will get a lot of wear and tear.

Quilts that are tied have a puffier look than those that are quilted. For extra puffiness, use a thick batting or even multiple layers of batting. For an added touch, sew buttons or other colorful ornaments onto the quilt top as you tie.

The best materials for tying are perle cotton, sport-weight yarn, or narrow ribbon. A tie is a stitch taken through all three layers of the quilt and knotted on the surface of the quilt top. In some cases, the knot is on the back.

To make a tie, from the right side of the quilt top, make a single running stitch through all layers, leaving a 3" tail (see Diagram 1). Make a single backstitch through the same holes formed by the running stitch (see Diagram 2).

Clip the thread, leaving a second 3" tail. Tie the clipped threads in a square knot close to the surface of the quilt (see Diagram 3). Don't pull the thread too tightly or it will create a pucker in the fabric.

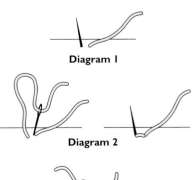

Diagram I

Diagram 2

Diagram 3

CREDITS

Quilt Designers

Alice Berg
Checkmate
Alice Berg of Marietta, Georgia, is one of three designers at Little Quilts. She enjoys replicating antique quilts.

Cindy Blackberg
Star Chain
Cindy Blackberg of Sorrento, Florida, enjoys teaching hand piecing and needle-turn appliqué.

Janet Carija Brandt
I Love You
Janet Carija Brandt of Indianapolis, Indiana, creates heirloom treasures using wool, felt, and cotton fabrics. Her work is strongly influenced by folk art.

Nora Cope
Crown of Thorns
Nora Cope of Rogers, Arkansas, is a former quilt shop owner. She favors scrap quilts and says "the trick is to get the colors to be pleasing, but not boring."

Helen Downing
Bella Tulip
Quiltmaker Helen Downing of Clive, Iowa, takes pleasure in hand piecing and hand appliquéing traditional quilt designs.

Bonnie Erickson and Joy Hoffman
American Beauty
When Bonnie Erickson (far left) of Granite Falls, Minnesota, and Joy Hoffman of Redwood Falls, Minnesota, collaborate on quilts, Joy does the piecing and Bonnie does the quilting.

Marty Freed
Sown Fabric
Marty Freed of Winterset, Iowa, creates quilts that tell stories for her family to enjoy.

Becky Goldsmith and Linda Jenkins
There Goes the Neighborhood
Pattern designers Linda Jenkins, *far left*, and Becky Goldsmith are partners in their own company, Piece O' Cake Designs.

Lynette Jensen
Lumberjack
Lynette Jensen of Hutchinson, Minnesota, is an author and designer of patterns and fabrics for her company, Thimbleberries, Inc.

Jackie Robinson
Durango Pinwheel
Jackie Robinson of Durango, Colorado, is a quilt designer, author, and a former quilt shop owner.

Mabeth Oxenreider
Timeless Treasure
Mabeth Oxenreider of Carlisle, Iowa, teaches quilting classes and challenges herself to create heirloom quilts using her sewing machine.

Jennifer Sampou and Carolie Hensley
Colorful Cakes
Carolie Hensley, *far left*, a quilt shop owner, and daughter-in-law Jennifer Sampou, a quilt designer, find collaborating on quilts to be a satisfying way to meld business and family relationships.

Nancy Slater
English Trellis
Nancy Slater of Turtle Lake, Wisconsin, is the owner of Wind in the Willows, a quilt shop featured in the 1999 issue of *Quilt Sampler* magazine.

Cleo Snuggerud
Candy Stripes
Cleo Snuggerud of Sioux Falls, South Dakota, enjoys creating simple, yet eye-catching projects for classes in her quilt shop, Heirloom Creations.

Darlene Zimmerman
Aunt Maggie's Quilt
Darlene Zimmerman of Fairfax, Minnesota, is a designer of quilts, fabrics, and quilting tools, as well as an author and teacher.

Quilt Tester
Laura Boehnke
Laura Boehnke of Garner, Iowa, created all the color options shown in this book. She is the quilt tester for *American Patchwork & Quilting* magazine.

Project Quilters and Finishers
Jan Bahr
Virginia Barker
Dot's Frame Shop
P. Edmond
Dorothy Faidley
Ruth A. Smith
Judy Sohn
Sally Terry
Kathleen Williams

Materials Suppliers
Benartex, Inc.
Fabri-Quilt, Inc.
Fairfield Processing Corp.
Hoffman Fabrics
Moda Fabrics
Northcott/Monarch
RJR Fashion Fabrics
Robert Kaufman Co.
Sulky of America

Photographers
Marcia Cameron: pages 28, 51, 60, 61, 62, 63, 73, 84, 87, and 107
Hopkins Associates: pages 8, 11, 102, 120, and 138
Scott Little: pages 55, 65, 88, 129, and 144
Perry Struse: pages 13, 15, 17, 21, 23, 24, 26, 29, 32, 36, 38, 41, 45, 47, 49, 51, 52, 58, 67, 68, 71, 75, 77, 78, 79, 81, 82, 85, 86, 92, 96, 99, 101, 109, 111, 115, 117, 124, 127, 131, 133, 135, 136, and 142
Steve Struse: pages 23, 37, 39, 43, 46, 53, 69, 79, 89, 106, 112, 115, 126, and 128